DEMOCRACY IN AFRICA

DEMOCRACY
in
AFRICA

BY
SIR IVOR JENNINGS
K.B.E., Q.C., Litt.D., LL.D., F.B.A.
Master of Trinity Hall, Cambridge
Bencher of Gray's Inn

CAMBRIDGE
AT THE UNIVERSITY PRESS
1963

CAMBRIDGE UNIVERSITY PRESS
Cambridge, New York, Melbourne, Madrid, Cape Town, Singapore,
São Paulo, Delhi, Dubai, Tokyo, Mexico City

Cambridge University Press
The Edinburgh Building, Cambridge CB2 8RU, UK

Published in the United States of America by Cambridge University Press, New York

www.cambridge.org
Information on this title: www.cambridge.org/9780521091961

© Cambridge University Press 1963

This publication is in copyright. Subject to statutory exception
and to the provisions of relevant collective licensing agreements,
no reproduction of any part may take place without the written
permission of Cambridge University Press.

First published 1963
Re-issued 2010

A catalogue record for this publication is available from the British Library

ISBN 978-0-521-09196-1 Paperback

Cambridge University Press has no responsibility for the persistence or
accuracy of URLs for external or third-party Internet Web sites referred to in
this publication, and does not guarantee that any content on such Web sites is,
or will remain, accurate or appropriate.

Preface

In 1955 the British Broadcasting Corporation asked me to deliver a series of talks discussing the problems which had arisen in the making of constitutions for India, Pakistan and Ceylon. An expanded version was published by the Syndics of the Cambridge University Press under the title *The Approach to Self Government*. Though the book was intended mainly for readers in the United Kingdom, it appears to have had a wide circulation in other parts of the Commonwealth, particularly in West, East and Central Africa.

Since 1955 there has been a vast accumulation of experience, not only in the three countries with which my talks were concerned, but also in Malaya, Singapore and Nepal, in the West Indies, in Ghana, Nigeria and Sierra Leone, in the Republic of Sudan, in the Federation of Rhodesia and Nyasaland, and in the four countries of East Africa, Kenya, Uganda, Tanganyika and Zanzibar. With some of the problems I have personally been concerned; others I have followed only from newspapers and white papers. These problems I tried to explain in a series of talks in the Overseas Service of the British Broadcasting Corporation early in 1961.

The occasion for the publication of this small book was, however, provided by a suggestion that there was need for a book on the political problems of emergent Africa, written in such a manner that it could be translated into some of the African languages. It seemed to me that this was a challenge which ought to be accepted, even though it involved an unusual effort of compression and simplification. As I knew from experience in Asia, one of the difficulties of making children literate in their own language is that there is often so little for them to read as adults. Even those who become literate in English, however, have difficulty in finding literature dealing directly with their own problems. It was therefore agreed, after discussion, that *Democracy in Africa* should be published in English and Hausa by the Cambridge University Press. It will, I hope, also be translated into other African languages.

It will therefore be appreciated by those who read the English version that it was written with translation in mind, and that the phrasing and imagery often reflect the probable difficulties of the translators rather than the difficulties of the subject. This may, however, help those who can read English but who are more fluent in their own languages.

In this book I have expressed my own opinions, derived from experience in many countries overseas and from discussions in which, from the official point of view, I was on the 'wrong' side of the table. It follows that these opinions bear no official imprint. The responsibility for all statements in the book is mine, and mine alone.

W.I.J.

TRINITY HALL
CAMBRIDGE
31 March 1962

Contents

		page	
	Preface	*page*	v
I	Africa and Western Culture		9
II	African Nationalism		25
III	Democracy		33
IV	The Social Order		43
V	Change in Africa		51
VI	Constitution-making		70
VII	The Aftermath		82

I. *Africa and Western Culture*

This books says very little about 'race' because it is a word of popular language which, like so many popular words, is found on careful analysis to have no precise meaning. When we speak of 'Europeans', 'Asians' and 'Africans' we mean people of European, Asian and African descent respectively. But this formula is very inexact. Throughout the known history of the world there have been migrations from one continent to another. Though there is a tendency for the migrants to keep to themselves for some generations, especially for purposes of marriage, there is a gradual mixture through intermarriage which in course of time produces fusion between the migrants and the indigenous people. This has been so especially in what may be called the Mediterranean world—Southern Europe, Western Asia and North Africa. It was for many centuries the centre of cultural development. It produced, for instance, Greek philosophy, Roman law, Arabic science and three of the world's great religions— Judaism, Christianity and Islam. But it was also a great centre of 'racial admixture'. Until the age of the railway, the macadamised road, and the motor vehicle, travel was always easier by water than by land; and so, though there were vast migrations by land, from which most of the peoples of Europe and many of those of Asia and Africa are descended, the land-locked and comparatively calm Mediterranean Sea made communication easy. Athens, Rome, Carthage, Alexandria, Istanbul, Jerusalem, Venice and Genoa were the great cities of history until cultural development moved to the eastern shores of the Atlantic, and that came about when the Ottoman Turks spread into the eastern Mediterranean. The sailors of Venice and Genoa taught the western peoples—the Spaniards, the Portuguese, the French, the Dutch and the English—to build larger ships and navigate the high seas. They had, probably, learned the technique from the Arabs of southern Asia, who dominated the Indian Ocean from the east coast of Africa to Indonesia until the Portuguese sailors rounded the southern tip of Africa.

If we think of these western peoples as 'Europeans', however, we must remember that, physiologically and culturally, they are very mixed. As an American historian of medieval Europe has put it: 'During periods as to which we have some knowledge, no race has continued pure from alien admixture; and every people that has taken part in the world's advance has been acted upon by foreign influences from its prehistoric beginnings throughout the entire course of its history. Indeed, foreign suggestions and contact with other peoples appear essential to tribal or national progress. For the historian there exists no pure and unmixed race, and even the conception of one becomes self-contradictory. To him a race is a group of people, presumably related in some way by blood, who appear to transmit from generation to generation a common heritage of culture and like physical and spiritual traits. He observes that the transmitted characteristics of such a group may weaken or dissipate before foreign influence, and much more as the group scatters among other people; or again he sees its distinguishing traits becoming clearer as the members draw to a closer national unity under the action of a common physical environment, common institutions, and a common speech. The historian will not accept as conclusive any single kind of evidence regarding race. He may attach weight to complexion, stature and shape of skull,[1] and yet find their interpretation quite perplexing when compared with other evidence, historical or linguistic. He will consider customs and implements, and yet remember that customs may be borrowed, and implements are often of foreign pattern. Language affords him the most enticing criterion, but one of the most deceptive. It is a matter of observation that when two peoples of different tongues meet together, they may mingle their blood through marriage, combine their customs, and adopt each other's utensils and ornaments; but the two languages will not structurally unite: one will supplant the other. The language may thus be more single in source than the people speaking it; though conversely, people of the same race, by reason of special circumstances, may not speak the same tongue. Hence linguistic unity is not conclusive evidence of unity of

---

[1] That is, to inherited physical characteristics.

Africa and Western Culture

race.'[1] In effect, a race is any group whose members believe themselves to be distinct. In this sense the peoples of Africa are of many races. The recent migrants from Europe and Asia tend, however, to treat the indigenous peoples—i.e. those whose ancestors have always lived in Africa or came to Africa with earlier migrations—as Africans and themselves as Europeans and Asians. That is, they generalise according to the continent of recent origin. This is a convenient usage merely because it is actually used in most parts of Africa. It is significant that it is not used where the migrations were recent but not very recent, i.e. over the whole area in which Arabic, Portuguese or Afrikaans is the spoken language. Where these complications do not exist, the usage is convenient because the Europeans, the Asians (i.e. the Indians, Pakistanis, etc.) and the Africans represent, speaking generally and with many exceptions due to cultural contacts, separate layers of social development.

The process by which the peoples of Western Europe, especially the Portuguese, the Spaniards, the French, the Dutch, the English, the Italians and the Germans, took the lead in social development is well known to historians because records are to be found not only in the vernacular languages but also in what used to be the common literary language of Western Europe, Latin.

Nine hundred years ago, all the territories which these people now occupy were parts of the great Roman Empire. Subsequently they were invaded by tribes which migrated from Eastern Europe and gradually overwhelmed the Roman Empire. The tribes seem to have been organised much like the migrant tribes from which so many of the peoples of Africa are descended.

They settled on the land and absorbed the indigenous peoples by inter-marriage. After settlement they were, to a greater or less extent, influenced by Roman culture. This is best illustrated by language. The Portuguese, the Spaniards, the French and the Italians use languages which were originally descended from Latin. The Dutch, the English and the Germans use languages which have developed out of the Germanic languages spoken by the later migrants, but the development was much helped by contacts with Roman culture. In the vast political changes which occurred in the thousand years after

[1] Henry Osborn Taylor, *The Mediaeval Mind* (4th ed.), vol. I, p.124.

the first invasions there was a continuous process of mixing cultures. For instance, the English language owes the richness of its vocabulary to the Norman occupation of England in the second half of the eleventh century after Christ. The Normans were Germanic invaders of Northern France who had settled down and became French-speaking. In the twelfth century, therefore, England was governed by a French-speaking class, though most of the peasants were English-speaking. Through inter-marriage the Normans and the English fused, so that by the fourteenth century English was the common language, though it had been much enriched by the inclusion of French words and expressions.

Also, though the Germanic tribes were culturally much less developed than the Romans, Roman influence upon them was continuous through the Christian Church, which continued to use Latin and to maintain some of the cultural traditions of Rome. The Church provided centres of Roman culture, some of which became universities in the thirteenth century. In these universities the whole field of knowledge could be studied, in so far as it could be found in Latin texts. In the fifteenth century the invention of printing in Germany made possible a much wider distribution of knowledge, not only in Latin, but also in the vernacular languages, which were continually being enriched by borrowing from Latin.

Much of the Roman culture had been taken from Greece, where a magnificent culture had developed in the centuries before Christ, strongly influenced by ideas imported from Asia and North Africa. The Roman Church itself had been founded on the Greek Churches and, while the Latin version of the books of the Old Testament was translated from Hebrew, the language of the Jews or Israelites, the books of the New Testament were translated from the Greek. St Paul, for instance, was a Roman citizen who spoke and wrote in Greek. A centre of Greek culture had been retained in Constantinople (now Istanbul) until the Turks captured the city in 1453. The Greek scholars thus migrated westwards soon after the invention of printing, and the combination threw open to the scholars of the West everything that remained of Greek culture.

Western culture was thus founded on the culture of Greece and Rome, though increasingly it was translated into the vernacular

Africa and Western Culture

languages, and thus became more widely available. Until the nineteenth century, however, every educated man in Europe had some knowledge of Latin and Greek. Latin remained the principal language of the universities until the eighteenth century,[1] but meanwhile the vernaculars, especially French and English, had become prolific instruments of cultural development. What is more, the advance of the Turks in Southern Europe and North Africa had pushed trade and commerce to North-Western Europe. The Portuguese and the Spaniards spread their influence to Central and South America; the French, the Dutch and the English spread their influence to North America. The Spaniards also spread to West Africa, where there are still Spanish colonies. The Portuguese rounded the Cape of Good Hope, sailed up the coast of East Africa, and across the Indian Ocean to India, Ceylon and Malaya. The Dutch, the French and the English followed. English sailors rounded Cape Horn and sailed into the Pacific Ocean, so that eventually British colonies were established in Australia and New Zealand.

These voyages were, however, comparatively small events in a major social and intellectual development, which would probably have been faster if it had not been for the dynastic wars in which most parts of Europe were involved by their ambitious sovereigns. The Portuguese and the Spaniards almost exhausted themselves. In the eighteenth century the lead was taken by the French; but the Bourbon monarchy, the French Revolution, Napoleon and other events of the period, reduced their potential. The most notable advances in technology were made by the British—as the English and the Scots had become by the Union of 1706. On the other hand, learning and intellectual development are not national characteristics. The use of Latin and French and, later, of English as international languages created a genuine 'commonwealth of learning' in Western Europe in which, in due course, people outside Western Europe participated. What interests modern Africa is not the particular contribution of each of the peoples but the whole *corpus* or body of knowledge which the peoples of Western Europe, and many outside—notably, in recent years, in the United States and the Union of Soviet Socialist Republics—have built up.

[1] It was a compulsory subject for all students of Oxford and Cambridge until 1960.

Democracy in Africa

It is no accident that this book is being written in one of the great centres of Western culture, one of those centres of the Roman Church which changed into universities. Around me as I write are the books of my private library. It is a 'working library' of perhaps five or six thousand volumes. Through the window, I can see the library of my College, covering a wider field and therefore perhaps ten times as large. From other rooms of my house I can see the tower of the great University Library, where there are millions of books in all the languages of the world. Even nearer to me, though not visible from my house, are the working libraries of the Faculties of Law and History. It is safe to say that within twenty minutes I could lay my hand on a copy of any significant work in any branch of knowledge. It does not follow that I could understand it, even if it were in English. So vast is now the range of knowledge that learned people have to be specialists. They are educated men and women who have devoted themselves to some branch of knowledge, received training in it, and acquired special skill in it. The greater part of the learning of the world is collected within half-a-mile of my house; but I can make use of it only in those particular branches of knowledge in which I have been trained.

Nevertheless, there are in Cambridge experts in all, or nearly all, branches of knowledge. Cambridge is, however, only one of the great centres of learning, scattered throughout the world, but especially in Western Europe and in those countries to which Western culture has been exported. They are not all universities. Some of the finest libraries are not university libraries but national libraries, like those in London, Paris and Washington. In all branches of knowledge there are specialist societies, sometimes national and sometimes international, which maintain libraries and publish periodicals. The great industries have their own research organisations and their own libraries. In short, there is a vast apparatus of learning, not specifically organised by anybody, and therefore called the 'commonwealth of learning', which has developed out of the progress of learning for the past five hundred years.

The really learned men and women are comparatively few, but some traces of this knowledge and experience spread to other sections of the population. Nearly everybody in Western Europe can read and write and most have completed at least eight years of school education. A labourer with this educational background is usually more skilled than one who is not. A skilled worker who has followed eight years of school with five years as an apprentice, a clerk who has had ten years of school education, an executive officer who has had twelve years of school education, and so forth, obviously have greater advantages and can take greater responsibilities than those who have not had this background.

It was, therefore, possible for the educated people of Western Europe to build up a culture which differed markedly from the relatively primitive cultures which had existed in the 'dark ages' between the fall of the Roman Empire and the rise of European culture. In the political field they created great nations with complicated systems of government. They improved agriculture by learning more about plants, animals and soil. They made better roads and bridges by learning more about mechanics. They built larger ships and sailed them all over the world. They invented printing and issued books in thousands. In course of time they built machines operated first by hand, then by steam, and then by electricity or oil. They invented steel and so made possible a new development of machinery. They made railways, huge steam-driven and oil-driven ships, motor cars, and aeroplanes. They invented concrete and erected huge buildings. In short, they made it possible to convert villages of mud huts into great cities like London, Paris and New York.

One ought not, however, to place too much stress on material changes. The building of nations and cities is evidence of development; and machinery enables the Europeans to maintain a high standard of living. But the foundation of the material structure is the stock of ideas set out in the books and taught in the schools and colleges. Generations of schoolboys must have wondered why so much that is taught at school seems to have so little relation to daily life. The answer is that they are mistaken. Subjects like mathematics, science, history, grammar, literature, and so forth are essential parts of the basis of culture, which does affect daily life. It is constantly being added to. Twenty thousand different books are published in England every year, and perhaps another twenty thousand are published in English in other English-speaking countries. The scale is not so large in other languages, but most educated people speak English as either first or second language, and most educated Englishmen can read at least one other European language, usually French. There is constant cross-fertilisation. There are differences of emphasis in London and in Paris, for instance, but any intellectual or artistic development in the one spreads very rapidly to the other. European culture is one though it is expressed in a dozen different languages.

There is one other factor in Western culture, of the greatest political importance. It may be called sympathy or compassion. It creates a sense of obligation towards one's fellow-men. Its origin was mainly Christian, for though European ethics came mainly from the Greeks, like much of European politics, the development of the Christian ideal—the ideal of the New Testament as against the ideal of the Old Testament—can be traced in the Latin writings of the medieval Christians and in Christian art. It has long ceased to be exclusively Christian. It is to be found in other religions, and in Western Europe itself it has been secularised. The fact that it is of Christian origin is, however, important because all the Christian churches have in consequence been, and still are, centres of propaganda for the idea of the brotherhood of man. When the human endeavour has fallen far behind the Christian ideal, as it often has done, the movement for reform has generally come from the churches. For instance, the movement for the abolition of the slave trade began in England with the Quakers and was taken up by politically more influential sections of the Church of England. It took a generation to persuade the British Parliament to make the slave trade illegal, and another generation to persuade it to buy out the slave-owners, so that all the slaves in the British dominions could be freed.

The importance of this factor in political development is that most of us believe that no system of government will succeed if it is founded purely on self-interest. Self-interest produces corrupt politicians, corrupt elections and, what is even worse in the long term, a wastage of natural resources. The conception of an obligation to humanity, both now and in future generations, is not necessarily Christian and it is possessed by man who are not Christians. It is, however, an essential feature of good government.

This book deals with those countries which either are now or have

Africa and Western Culture

been in the recent past under British rule. Because of that rule they have been influenced by British ideas. The language which they use for cultural development is English, their laws—apart from religious or customary laws—are founded on English law; their political institutions are based on British political institutions; their schools and university colleges are copied or adapted from English models. This interchange of 'English' and 'British' is perhaps confusing, but it can be explained simply. England was the home of the language, and though it spread into Wales and Scotland it has never been called British, because it has not completely driven out the local languages. Educationally too, England and Scotland have always differed, partly because in the sixteenth and seventeenth centuries Scotland was closely associated with France and Holland. The laws of England and Scotland differ for the same reason. When in 1603 the King of Scotland became King of England, the laws and the political institutions of England and Scotland remained different. In 1706, however, the Parliaments of the two countries agreed upon a union. The Queen of England and Scotland became Queen of Great Britain. Her English and Scottish subjects became British subjects. To the Parliament of England were added representatives from Scotland, and it became the Parliament of Great Britain. The Queen's Government became the British Government. The term 'British' was retained when the United Kindom of Great Britain and Ireland (since 1927 the United Kingdom of Great Britain and Northern Ireland) was created in 1801. Hence British people brought to Africa the English language, English law, schools and universities on English models, but British political institutions.

Development along modern lines began in Africa as soon as the first Europeans arrived. Foreigners stimulate new ideas whether their purpose is nefarious like that of the slave-traders, or beneficial like that of the missionaries. Until late in the nineteenth century, however, British influence in the interior of Africa was small. Their trading posts in West Africa became small 'colonies'—Bathurst in the Gambia, Freetown and its neighbourhood in Sierra Leone, the narrow strip of the Gold Coast, and a small area around Lagos. These territories were, to use the legal expression, annexed to the British Crown. They became British territories and their inhabitants became British subjects. The later developments were effected not by extending British territory but by offering British protection to the tribal authorities. Though some British people had wider ambitions, it was not the intention of any British Government to subvert local institutions or to establish British institutions. Its purpose was to suppress the slave trade, exercise control over European and Asian traders, and keep out other European powers.

In the present century, however, the distinction between 'colonies' and 'protectorates' has almost disappeared. Protection was found to involve the making of roads and bridges, the erection of schools, hospitals and clinics, the stimulation of forestry and agriculture, and the provision of a whole apparatus of government of which the tribal authorities became part. For this there were several reasons. Some roads and some bridges had to be built for protective purposes. A tribe could hardly be protected if it could not be reached except after a trek of days or weeks through the bush. But roads and bridges opened up the country, stimulated trade, and encouraged Africans as well as others to produce crops for sale. This in turn encouraged more roads and more bridges, more trade, and so forth in a regular cycle. From this 'opening up', too, came a demand for medical, veterinary and agricultural services, and the development of an apparatus of government. What is more, all this required money. Until 1940, nearly all of it had to come from local sources. Poll taxes, house taxes, etc., brought in little revenue, but increased trade brought increased customs duties.

If a stone is rolled down a bare hillside, it dislodges other stones, and every stone so dislodged dislodges other stones, so that not one stone but a cascade of stones reaches the bottom of the hill. So it was in the protectorates. The distinction between the Gold Coast Colony and the Gold Coast Protectorate became increasingly unreal as the Protectorate was opened up to trade and the production of cocoa and bananas developed. In Nigeria the development came later; but once it started it went very fast indeed as the demand for palm oil and cotton increased. In Southern Rhodesia and Kenya there was an even more important factor, the settlement of European farmers in some parts of the countryside. They knew from experience in Europe or South Africa or Canada or Australia that to make land productive it was necessary to spend money on it, to drain it or irrigate it, to manure it, to import or produce better stock and better seed, and so forth. They employed local labour on the land, but they also set up a demand for agricultural implements, stone or brick, cement, European clothes, food and drink, and so forth, which in turn required more local labour. The Africans so employed were paid wages which they spent on commodities which they needed. They, too, stimulated trade, and so created employment.

In short, once development started it proceeded at an increasing pace. It depended, however, on two factors outside the African territories. First, it depended on a continually increasing demand for tropical products—cocoa, bananas, cotton, coffee, tea, tobacco, sisal, and so forth— in the great centres of population, mainly in Europe and America. Secondly, it depended on the willingness of investors in other countries, especially in Britain, to invest in enterprises in Africa which were likely to bring profit to themselves and would undoubtedly bring employment to Africans. The capital so invested had to come from outside because it always consists of savings, the difference between what is earned and what is spent. Poor men have little or no capital because they need to spend all they earn. In due course, as the economy develops, poor men become richer and accumulate savings, or capital. The process has to begin, however, with imported capital, which may provide for the actual production of goods (for instance, by clearing bush and planting cocoa or coffee) and certainly must provide for transport, harbour facilities, warehouses, banks, insurance, and all the other facilities required by an export trade.

In 1929 there was a rapid decrease both in the demand for tropical products and in the provision of capital for African development. The 'depression' began in the United States of America and spread to Europe. Millions of men were out of work and millions of others had their incomes reduced. They could not afford to buy as much African produce, and prices fell. Even those who had capital feared that its employment in Africa would be unprofitable. Consequently, not only was African development halted, but it actually went backwards. Africans who depended on jobs in the fields, in the mines, in the shops, or elsewhere, found themselves unemployed and destitute. If they had homes to which they could return they depressed an already very low standard of living.

The British Government had already appreciated that the financing of development by local taxes and private capital was not entirely satisfactory, and in 1929 a Colonial Development Fund was established to make grants and loans to Colonial Governments for development purposes. The amounts of money available were small, the use of the money was rigidly limited, and, of course, the loans had to be repaid. The West Indies probably suffered most from the great depression, and in 1938 their social and economic conditions were investigated by a Royal Commission. As a result, a new policy of helping colonial development and welfare by grants from the British Treasury was adopted in 1940 and is still in operation. Not all the schemes have been equally successful. Nevertheless, the colonial development and welfare grants have added pace to the speed at which African developments have taken place since 1945. Though there have been trade fluctuations since then, conditions generally have improved, by increased production, increased trade, increased investment, increased government expenditure, and increased employment.

Once again, we must not lay too much stress on economic development. It is, of course, fundamentally important, but economic development cannot proceed very far in Africa unless there are men and women capable of making use of new opportunities. Social development and economic development have to go together. That, indeed, is why 'development' is linked with 'welfare'. It is necessary to improve the men and women, partly by education and partly by improving the conditions in which they live. These things react on each other. Education teaches, for instance, about the pollution of water, and when steps are taken to prevent pollution the children of the next generation are physically more capable of receiving education. The eradication of the diseases which were once common, like cholera, smallpox, typhoid, malaria and hookworm, has had great effects even in our lifetime. People used to write books about villages which gradually declined and died until they became mere mounds in the bush. There were no old men and women in such villages because they died young; but the older men and women looked very, very old

Africa and Western Culture

because, in the conditions in which they lived, they aged very quickly. Even the young were weak and listless because none were free of disease; and they were an easy prey to the occasional epidemics. Probably there are still such villages in the remoter parts of Africa, and certainly there are villages which, on the standards of Western Europe or even on the best standards of Asia, are very, very bad. On the other hand, there are villages full of lively and intelligent people whose future is assured.

It is not enough to have schools and to teach in them the elementary notions of public heath. We know how to make a village healthy because so many generations have studied the medical sciences; and they could study the medical sciences because they had studied the natural sciences; and they could study the natural sciences because they had absorbed the learning of Greece and Rome and the rest of the ancient world. When we try to get to the root of any African problem we meet, in the end, the millions of books which surround me as I write. In other parts of the world there are great traditions and a mass of accumulated knowledge, but they too are to be found in the millions of books—the languages and literature of Asia and Africa, the great religions of Asia, the relics of ancient civilisation in Asia, Africa and America. There are, too, great libraries in most parts of the world. In a matter like this we tend to revert to the Latin and to speak of the *corpus* of knowledge, the body or integrated collection of knowledge which has been made and expanded in Western Europe, and more recently in Eastern Europe, in Asia, and in America. We are, it is true, only on the fringes of knowledge. What we know is probably only a fraction of what our successors will know. But what Africa needs is full and free access to the *corpus* of knowledge, and this can come only through education.

This raises difficult problems. The *corpus* of knowledge is adequately displayed only in the major languages of Europe. Those languages have grown as knowledge has grown. Even the greater languages of Asia, which are highly developed and have ancient literatures, need further development before they can be effectively used for the whole *corpus* of knowledge. They can be developed by artificial means, such as the invention of scientific and other terms for ideas which have never before been expressed in those languages.

Democracy in Africa

Even then the *corpus*, or a substantial part of it, has to be translated. Osmania University in India was given money for the translation of standard text-books into Urdu. After 25 years they had translated only 500 books. I looked at the list and found that in my subject every book was out of date. In England alone in those 25 years something like 250,000 books must have been published, and there are millions of books in the *corpus* of knowledge.

In Africa there are hundreds of different languages, some of them very primitive, some quite advanced: but none are advanced enough to express the whole *corpus* of knowledge. It would take a long time and much effort to develop them. Even when they had been developed, a substantial section of the *corpus* of knowledge would have to be translated. This is being done in Arabic-speaking countries, for Arabic is an advanced language and the Arabs of former generations had contributed notably to the *corpus* of knowledge. Even so, it is necessary for Arabic-speaking people to be able at least to read either English or French. In the rest of Africa education has to be wholly or partially in a European language, English in the British Commonwealth and French in the former French colonies.

It is of course true, as I have said already, that nobody can get to know the whole of the *corpus* of knowledge. We have to specialise. Some of us are parsons, some lawyers, some physicians and surgeons, some scientists, some economists, and so on. What is more, those of us who go to universities are a minority. Even in a highly developed country like the United Kingdom only about one student in twenty goes to a university, and an African country could manage with even fewer. Indeed a country which could provide university education for one in every hundred boys and girls would do remarkably well. Nevertheless, unless a country can recruit expatriate specialists, it has to provide its own in every field of activity. Such provision can be made only if there are many people being educated up to the Higher School Certificate, many more being educated to the level of the School Certificate, and almost the whole of the child population receiving at least six years of school education. The educational structure has to be like a high hill, with the university students at the narrow top and the primary school students at the broad base.

The problem of language is not the only problem. It is generally agreed that except where in-breeding lowers the standard of intelligence—as it does in small isolated communities in all parts of the world—ability is evenly spread in the different countries. The difficulty with which African students have often to contend is not lack of ability but lack of 'background'. Only a part of education is given in school. The rest comes from a student's family, his friends, his general reading, his activities outside school, and his social surroundings generally. Educated parents do not necessarily produce abler sons than uneducated parents, but they can give their sons a better home education by talking to them and to each other. Boys who are in the first generation of literates in English on the average do less well than boys in the second generation of literates in English, who in turn do less well, on the average, than boys in the third generation of literates in English. Three generations of literates are rare in tropical Africa, and even two generations are not very common.

This is, however, only one aspect. An English boy (to take him as an example) not only belongs to the fourth generation of literates at least—he might belong to the twentieth—but so do his friends, with whom he plays. At home he has access to newspapers and magazines, and probably his family has a private library. Even if there are no books at home, there is a public library nearby from which he can borrow books. Moreover, his family probably listens regularly to wireless broadcasts, or regularly watches television. These introduce children when still very young to a range of ideas which they would not otherwise meet either at home or at school. In many homes, too, there are gramophones and pianos. In large towns there are cinemas, theatres, concerts, museums and art galleries. There is an enormous range of activity which impresses itself on the boy or the girl without anybody noticing it particularly.

An African boy acquires knowledge of which a European boy is probably profoundly ignorant. There are, too, Africans of deep culture as well as of great ability. In all the African territories of the Commonwealth there is an *élite* of educated Africans. It is small by European standards and even by Asian standards, and it needs to be enlarged as quickly as possible. The means for doing so are now available in schools and university colleges. For the time being, however, there are great difficulties in finding staff to provide the services of a modern society; and these difficulties are increased by the fact that the general population, for whom those services are provided, have so little of the knowledge and experience required to improve their own conditions. The remaining chapters of this book seek to explain some of these difficulties in the sphere of government.

II. *African Nationalism*

Nationalism is one of the ideas exported by Europe. The tribes which brought about the fall of the Roman Empire settled on the land, intermarried with such of the local people as they did not drive out, and became the present European peoples. The tribal system as such died out and was gradually replaced by what the historians call the feudal system. Though its characteristics differed in different places, its essence was that a village or a group of villages was in control of a 'lord' who was for all practical purposes owner of the land. The lord owed duties to a superior lord, who might in the developed system be called a count (or earl), a duke or a king. If he was a count or a duke he in turn owed duties to a king. These respective duties included a duty of loyalty called 'allegiance'. In the system which the feudal lawyers described, every villager owed a duty of loyalty to his lord, every lord to his count or earl, every count or earl to his duke, and every duke to his king. The system never operated in this way in practice, because the realities of power were more important than the formalities of law; and when the system died out the only loyalty left was the loyalty to the king.

This personal duty of the subject to the king was the foundation of national duty or patriotism. It was easily extended from the king personally to the state or country—from King Edward or Henry to England, and thence to Great Britain, and finally to the United Kingdom. The state is treated as a person, to whom loyalty and affection are due by its citizens; and loyalty and affection require duty and service. It is a privilege to be a citizen, but it implies a duty also, a duty to be a loyal, useful and worthy citizen.

Similar developments occurred, rather later, in other parts of Europe, and now the system is world-wide. The people of a nation do not necessarily speak the same language. In the United Kingdom Welsh and Gaelic, as well as English, are spoken. In Belgium there are two languages and in Switzerland there are four. There has, however, been a tendency for people speaking the same language to regard themselves as kin and to want to get together in the same nation. Italy and Germany were formed on this basis, though there are Italian-speaking people in Switzerland and German-speaking people in Switzerland, Austria and even Italy. The theory of kinship is of course plain nonsense. All the peoples of the world are as mixed as the Americans, whose mixture is recent and therefore more obvious. They speak English because many of the early settlers were English, and their language became the language of communication among the settlers from many countries. The Italian emigrant tends to speak Italian to his wife and English to his children, because the children will have to make careers among English-speaking people. It is obviously absurd to suggest that everybody who speaks English is English by descent. Indeed, it is hard to find anybody who is exclusively English by descent, for migration is continuous, especially from Wales, Scotland, Ireland and the Commonwealth overseas.

Nevertheless, nationalism has a strong emotional content. As we have seen, it began in Europe as allegiance or loyalty to a king. It is easy to develop loyalty to a wise or brave leader, but especially so when he has the dignity of a king, and even more so when he leads his armies in warfare, as the English kings did in the fourteenth and fifteenth centuries. Wars always help to stimulate loyalty; indeed, they tend to turn patriotism into its more aggressive forms. There are, however, more attractive elements in patriotism. The word itself comes from the Latin word for 'father', and in many languages the word for one's country has to be translated 'fatherland'. The sentimental English more often use 'motherland'. Similarly, the language which one learns at home is often called the 'mother-tongue'. Sometimes the English and the Germans refer to the 'homeland'. What all this means is that the affection and self-sacrifice that are normal in happy families are attached to the country or the nation. The adult, worn with the cares of the world, remembers his childhood when (as he thinks) he was carefree. He feels sentimental about his country just as he feels sentimental about his home. He is also sentimental about his language. He learned to speak it at his mother's knee; he learned to read and write it at school; he has continued to read its literature ever since, and much of that literature, especially its poetry, stimulates the emotions. Sometimes, though, the country and the language are not the same. Where two or more languages are spoken, the sentiment for the language may be greater than the sentiment for the nation. There are, too, other factors which may divide a nation. Religion may be one. There may be a division between Christians and Muslims, or even between Roman Catholics and Protestants. Where the tribal system persists, there may be a conflict of loyalties between the nation and the tribe.

If nationalism is aggressive, as it often is when dictators seize power, it is a threat to the peace of the world. A dictator tends to divert the criticism of his own actions by attacking somebody else. He then capitalises nationalist sentiment by directing it against the 'enemy'. In a genuine democracy, on the other hand—and we shall see presently what that means—nationalism in the mild form called patriotism is a useful quality. As I shall explain presently, government is not just a process in which the rulers give orders to those who are ruled. The rulers have objectives which are acceptable to the people, whom they represent, and they need and expect the collaboration of the people. When the Parliament of the United Kingdom makes laws, it assumes that people will obey them because they are sensible laws; and if anybody disagrees with the aims of a law it is still his duty to obey because, if some laws are not obeyed, many other laws will not be obeyed. There are, of course, people who do break laws. Not only are they punished when tried and convicted, but also they are regarded by ordinary people as offenders against society. Nor is it only a question of laws. To serve the state (or, as it would be put in most parts of the Commonwealth, to serve the Queen) is both a privilege and a duty. It was a Roman who said that it was sweet and glorious to died for one's fatherland; but many patriots in many countries have not hesitated to die, and many things can be done for one's country short of dying.

Though hardly anybody in Europe remembers it, states are artificial creations. They are products of history. A man is 'French' or 'German' because he happens to have been born on the one side or the other of a line drawn more or less arbitrarily on a map. In fact, there was a long conflict over the question whether two provinces, Alsace and Lorraine, should be on the one side of the line or the other. Switzerland, Luxembourg and Belgium were created comparatively recently. Language sometimes determines state boundaries, but often it does not. French is spoken in Belgium, Luxembourg and Switzerland as well as in France. German is spoken in Switzerland and Austria as well as in Germany. English is the language, or one of the languages, of a score of nations. In fact, language tends to follow the boundary; not the boundary follow the language. French was taught in Alsace and Lorraine until 1870, when the two provinces became German; German was then taught until 1918, when they became French; and French has been taught since 1918.

It is therefore not very important that most of the boundaries of Africa are recent. They were due to the accident that the Portuguese, the Spaniards, the French, the British, the Germans, the Italians or the Belgians established posts in the territories, that the boundaries were subsequently drawn by a series of agreements among the colonial powers, and that sometimes the colonial powers, as in French West Africa, divided the territories for administrative convenience. If the boundaries were redrawn on a geographical or ethnical basis it is certain that the curious medley of states in West Africa would not exist. One cannot, however, rewrite history. Ghana is an entity because it was formerly the Gold Coast Colony and Protectorate. It may be possible, as it was in Nigeria, to divide a territory into 'regions'. It may be possible, as has been suggested both in West and in East Africa, to secure agreements for the union of two or more territories. It is not very easy to secure such agreements, because history creates vested interests. Though England and Scotland had the same king and most of the Scots spoke English, it took a hundred years to persuade them to unite. What is more, there were obvious advantages to *both* countries in a union. Nor were there politicians or civil servants who would lose jobs if a union were formed, as there probably would be in Africa.

The difficulty of securing agreement for closer union has been shown in the West Indies. They consist of a number of islands scattered over a very wide area, each with its own characteristics. Efforts to secure closer union among some or all of the islands have been going on for nearly three hundred years. Until 1932, however, there was little chance of securing agreement to a federation of most, if not all, of the islands. That date is significant. It was the end of a great depression in which the West Indies had suffered particularly severely from unemployment. It was felt by many that the only way to improve economic conditions was to have a larger unit which would not only provide a substantial home market, but also organise the export trade more efficiently and so provide against unemployment and low wages. It was felt, too, that if the islands were federated it would be easier to secure self-government. These very strong economic and political arguments had nevertheless to overcome opposition from vested interests, ignorance and apathy among substantial sections of the population, and the parochial attitudes which so often develop in small communities. A federation was at last established in 1957, but it broke up in 1962 and plans for a less comprehensive federation had to be discussed.

The purpose of a federation is to secure 'union without unity'; that is, the purpose is to enable a central government to operate in matters of common concern, while leaving local governments to operate in matters of local concern. Among the matters of common concern are defence and external relations, because these require very expensive services whose cost ought to be spread over as wide an area as possible. Other services which are almost invariably common are currency, telecommunications, air services, railways, postal services, and research. Usually, however, the main purpose is economic. A small country with few natural resources finds it difficult to maintain even essential services and virtually impossible to raise the capital needed for economic development. It is as easy for a rich country to become richer as it is for a rich man to become richer; and it is just as difficult for a poor country to become richer as it is for a poor man to become richer. Neither the poor country nor the poor man has the capital needed for enrichment; and neither can they borrow because lenders want to be assured that they will get their money back, with interest. Even a small country like Sierra Leone, Northern Rhodesia or Southern Rhodesia has a reasonable chance of development if it has easily accessible natural resources in great demand overseas. Even such a country can, however, hope for more rapid development if it forms part of a larger whole. The economic arguments for the creation of the Federation of Rhodesia and Nyasaland were very strong, and it was hoped in 1953 that the advantages of the Federation would become so obvious that its continuance would be generally acceptable. Events have shown, however, that large sections of African opinion in the territories were not prepared to support it. The case for closer union in East Africa is equally strong. Indeed, important services are already provided by the East African High Commission; and any attempt to raise living standards by cooperative action would require the provision of more common services. The experience of history is that such services cannot for long be provided by agreement.

In this respect nationalism is something of an impediment. If one gets used to the notion that Nyasaland or Tanganyika is a separate 'country', it is difficult to persuade patriotic citizens to submerge their patriotism in a larger patriotism, to think of Central Africa rather than Nyasaland, or East Africa rather than Tanganyika. Moreover, personalities enter into the matter. If the 'nation' is enlarged, which of the present leaders will become leaders and which will become lieutenants? Thus, the further nationalism percolates the more difficult it is to secure broad agreements which will lead to economic development on a large scale.

Even so, it takes time for patriotic sentiments to spread among all sections of the people, especially where there are differences of religion, language, race or tribe. The union of Great Britain and Ireland was never a success because the Roman Catholics of Southern Ireland thought of themselves not as British but as Irish. In most of the newly independent territories, formerly British, in Asia there is a conflict between nationalism and what is called 'communalism'. In Ceylon, for instance, there was a large middle-class minority of English-speaking Ceylonese. They were strongly nationalist both before and after independence. They thought of themselves as Ceylonese and for forty years they agitated for self-government. From them were chosen the nominated and elected members of the Legislative Council. Some of them became Ministers in 1931 and, when independence was attained in 1948, all the Ministers and members of Parliament, as well as all the senior civil servants, were English-speaking. On the other hand, this nationalism did not go very deep among the rest of the population. There were religious differences because there were Buddhists, Hindus, Muslims and Christians. There were language differences because some spoke Sinhalese and some spoke Tamil. There were differences which were thought to be racial, because, though the Sinhalese and the Tamils, like all other so-called 'races', were mixed, there had been very little inter-marriage in recent generations. There were educational differences, because some had been educated through Sinhalese and some through Tamil; and this was not solely a difference of language because, for instance, the Sinhalese history of Ceylon is different from the Tamil history of Ceylon, though both agreed that there had been a long conflict between the Sinhalese and the Tamils. It was, therefore, easy for those Sinhalese or Tamil politicians who found themselves excluded from power by the nationalist groups, who had taken over in 1948, to appeal to the 'communal' sentiments of the Sinhalese or the Tamils. The Sinhalese politicians succeeded in becoming Ministers, but they also stimulated communal antagonism, which led to serious rioting. For several days in 1958 the country was in a state of anarchy. Fortunately, the army remained loyal and, under the personal direction of the Governor-General, re-established law and order.

The sort of sectionalism which is called 'communalism' in Asia is generally called 'tribalism' in Africa, because it is usually founded upon tribal institutions. We must, of course, remember that nationalism and tribalism are not necessarily in conflict. In every state there are differences among the people which have to be recognised, accepted and indeed honoured. The Welsh and the Scots are loyal to their own countries but manage to get on with the English. What went wrong in Ceylon was not that some Ceylonese were loyal Sinhalese but that ambitious politicians roused the Sinhalese so much that they attacked the Tamils. In India the Congress Party properly insists that a good Bengali must not be a bad Indian. In other words, the local, religious, communal or tribal sentiment must be made part of the wider patriotic sentiment. Just as the British never convinced most of the Irish Roman Catholics, so the Indian National Congress never convinced most of the Indian Muslims. Since 1947, however, the Congress 'high command' has insisted that, though most Indians are Hindus, India must be a secular state because the religions of those who are not Hindus must be respected. Similarly, though India needs a national language, all the languages and cultures of India must be encouraged.

In the same way, tribal traditions can be maintained even in a democratic state. Perhaps the Federation of Malaya provides a better analogy than India. There the Malays, who are only half the population, have a strong sentimental attachment to their Rulers, of whom there are nine. Clearly a comparatively small country like Malaya can no longer be divided into nine independent states, each governed autocratically by a Ruler. But this does not necessarily mean that the Rulers must be pensioned off, as the Indian Maharajahs were. They have been fitted into a democratic constitution as 'constitutional rulers' like the Queen of the United Kingdom and given all the honours and dignity that the Malays would wish them to have. At the same time, the Malay political leaders have insisted that every Malayan, be he Malay, Chinese or Indian, must regard himself as a loyal Malayan citizen. Whether such an arrangement will succeed is in the hands of history. It may be that, as in Ceylon, future politicians will find it convenient to arouse communal sentiments by setting the Malays against the Chinese. The present intention is, however, to provide an even broader foundation by incorporating the Federation of Malaya, Singapore, North Borneo, Sarawak and Brunei in a single political entity to be called Malaysia. The moral is plain. Sectional loyalties must be respected because they are strong and traditional; but a new national loyalty must also be developed, so that sectional loyalty never conflicts with national loyalty.

III. *Democracy*

There are several forms of democratic government; and also there are several forms of government which are called democratic, especially by communists, because 'democracy' is now one of those pleasure-giving words like 'peace', 'prosperity', 'happiness', and 'independence'. Fifty years ago, when a child was not feeling well, he was given a spoonful of 'jam'. It looked like jam; it tasted like jam; and it was jam; but it also contained a pill or a powder which, taken by itself, tasted quite horrid. The jam was a disguise for the pill or the powder. So 'democracy' often hides the reality of power exercised by some person or group of persons trying to maintain himself or themselves in power. That the jam contains a pill or powder is often indicated by the fact that two pleasure-giving words are placed together. A 'people's democracy' or a 'peace-loving democracy' is certain to be a communist dictatorship, a 'true democracy' or a 'controlled democracy' is probably a military or a bureaucratic dictatorship.

Since most of my readers will be familiar with the British type of democracy, I propose to discuss that particular form. I shall have to qualify my statements presently, but the essence of British democracy may be stated as follows:

(1) The right to vote (or the franchise) is exercisable by every person aged 21 or more, freely and secretly.

(2) Representation in the House of Commons is roughly equal; that is to say, every member of the House of Commons has been elected for a 'constituency' based as far as possible on a population of 90,000.

(3) No law may be made unless it is approved by a majority of the members of the House of Commons, sitting and voting.

(4) The government in power is responsible to the House of Commons, i.e. it cannot exist unless it has the continuous support of the majority of the members of the House of Commons.

Democracy in Africa

There are 630 members of the House of Commons, and so there are 630 constituencies. Every five years, or more often if the Queen on the advice of her Prime Minister so decides, there has to be a general election, i.e. an election in each of the 630 constituencies. It is now unusual to have uncontested elections, and so there are two, three, or even four candidates in each constituency. The great majority of them are party candidates, prepared to support a Conservative Government, or a Liberal Government, or a Labour Government. Hence, if a Conservative Government is in office and a majority of Labour members is elected the Government must resign forthwith so that the Queen may appoint a Labour Government. In other words, the continuance of the Government in power depends upon the judgment of the electors in the 630 constituencies, expressed freely and secretly.

This judgment is based not on personalities but on political principles. Each party tries to make plain the principles on which it proposes to act if it secures a majority. Each candidate stresses those principles in his electioneering. The Government, as such, takes no part in electioneering, though the members of the Government do so as members of their party. This may not seem a very clear distinction, but in fact it is very clear because public funds may not be used for electioneering. A Conservative Government is Her Majesty's Government and spends money in Her Majesty's name. It would be quite improper to spend that money on securing the election of its members. The money spent by Conservative Ministers is party money, collected privately from supporters of the party, and none of it comes from public funds.

If a Conservative Government is in office and the Conservative party fails to obtain a majority, the members of that party in the two Houses of Parliament go into 'opposition'; and so, facing Her Majesty's Government is 'Her Majesty's Opposition'. That name was given as a joke more than 150 years ago, but it has been retained because it indicates a profound truth, that Her Majesty's Government requires an Opposition to criticise the Government's actions and policies, in order that the electors may make a choice between rival policies and therefore between competing parties. Not all democracies follow this particular pattern; but it is an abuse of language to

Democracy

describe as a 'democracy' any system of government in which there are not at least two parties, each of which has equal facilities for appealing to the people and which may be freely supported by any elector. That knocks out all fictitious 'people's democracies', 'controlled democracies', and what not.

Since most African politicians in British dependencies want this particular type of democracy, I must emphasise that it has been evolved to suit the conditions in the United Kingdom and not to support any particular political theory. It rests upon assumptions which I cannot attempt to expound in a single chapter:[1] but I can mention some of the former or existing qualifications.

The Franchise

The present franchise was not adopted until 1948, and it is based fundamentally on the individualist nature of British society. I have mentioned how the tribal society of the Anglo-Saxons became the feudal society of the Anglo-Normans. That feudal society settled down into a well-ordered system in which, outside the towns, power and influence depended on the ownership of land. Even the towns, if they were small enough, were under the influence of neighbouring landowners. The constituencies were the counties and the towns (boroughs); and each sent two members to Parliament irrespective of size. The result was that, for three hundred years, the landowners governed England. In a county every landowner had the vote, but the smaller (or peasant) landowners accepted the choice of the great men. In a borough the franchise might be wide or narrow, but generally the choice of the neighbouring landowners was accepted.

This system was much criticised in the nineteenth century, but it accorded with the social structure until the industrialisation of Great Britain began. In other words, it became ill-suited to the conditions only when those conditions changed. Factories using steam-power attracted population into the towns. The landowners continued to dominate the agricultural counties until 1885, but no landowner could adequately represent a great city like Birmingham or Manchester. The franchise was therefore reformed, but in five steps at intervals of a generation. The first reform, that of 1832, balanced

[1] See Sir Ivor Jennings, *The British Constitution* (4th ed.).

urban and rural representation. It also abolished the representation of the very small towns (which became parts of their counties) and provided for representation of the new industrial towns. In the counties, leaseholders as well as landowners were given the vote provided that they paid a substantial rent; and in the boroughs a householder was given the vote provided that he occupied a large enough house. In other words, the landed interest and the new urban middle class shared the representation.

In 1867 every householder in a town was enfranchised, and so working-men shared urban representation with the middle class; and this was extended to the counties in 1884-5. By this time, Britain was primarily an industrial country, for even land came to be regarded as a commodity to be bought and sold. The deference which had traditionally been paid to the squire or large landowner in the 'big house' was disappearing, and in many places had already disappeared. The town, not the village, was the characteristic feature of the social system, and the typical family was the urban household, consisting of parents and minor children, and not the 'patriarchal' family on the land, i.e. the grandfather, his sons, his grandsons and their respective wives. The wealthy man was no longer primarily a landowner, for he was interested in stocks and shares. The poorer man was no longer helping to cultivate his father's land; he was an employee in the city.

By 1918 the individual, not the family, was the essential unit, and so the logical step was taken of giving the vote to every male of 21 years of age or more. At the same time, the women of 30 years of age or more were enfranchised. Until late in the 19th century nobody thought that women should have the vote, because they were represented by their fathers or their husbands. Their social position had been changing, however, partly because of the growing individualisation of society—the son's wife no longer deferred to her mother-in-law—but mainly because of the development of popular education. Popular education developed rapidly after 1832, and even more rapidly after 1870, when for the first time schools were provided by local education authorities. In 1881 primary education was made compulsory and in 1891 it was made free. By 1918 the whole adult population was literate and, indeed, had had at least seven years of

Democracy

school education. The wife was as educated as her husband. The war of 1914-18 completed the emancipation of women, because so many men were in the armed forces that a great many jobs had to be undertaken by women. This emancipation was shown by the adoption of what most Africans who have contact with Europeans would now regard as the typical costume of European women (though it dates only from 1915), the short frock, the trimmed hair, and the hatless head. The elaborate gowns, coiffures and hats of the nineteenth century became impracticable when women led a more active life. The change in social conventions, illustrated by this change of costume, made it inevitable that women should have the franchise on the same terms as men, though the change was not complete until 1928.

Even in 1945, however, there were still relics of older ideas. Until 1918 there were several different qualifications, so that a man might have several votes. After 1918 nobody was allowed to exercise more than two; and in 1948 only the simple residential qualification was allowed. The United Kingdom had reached the principle of 'one man (or woman), one vote'.

This interpretation of the franchise laws in terms of social structure is slightly exaggerated. During the whole period the United Kingdom had something like party government, and naturally each of the political parties considered how far an extension of the franchise would affect its support in the constituencies. In 1832 the Whigs thought that the enfranchisement of the new towns would increase their representation as against the Tory landowners. In 1867 the Conservatives hoped that the urban householders would vote Conservative because their employers were usually Liberals. In 1884-5 the Liberals believed that rural householders would support them against Conservative landlords. In 1918 and 1948 the changes were based mainly on agreements between the parties.

Even so, the close relationship between the franchise on the one hand and social and educational development on the other needs to be emphasised. So long as the whole village deferred to the squire it was quite adequately represented by the squire's nominee, just as a College is represented by its Master or a trade union by its leaders. The obligations were of course mutual, for the squire did his best for his tenants, in bad times as well as in good. But no squire could represent Birmingham. What is more, the franchise tended to follow political education. In most parts of the country the urban householders were actively interested in political questions for a generation before 1867, but this did not apply in the rural areas until the old paternalistic village broke up through the influx of cheap American corn and the development of scientific agriculture. As soon as the squire became a profit-making farmer he ceased to be the 'father' of the village and could no longer represent the villagers.

Constituencies

The old idea of representation was that each 'community', i.e. each county and borough, should be separately represented. These counties and boroughs were ancient social as well as administrative units. The idea was never fully carried out because some of the boroughs had been created for political purposes in the sixteenth and seventeenth centuries; and social changes since 1660 had by 1830 increased the element of fiction in the theory of representation. Even in 1832, however, it was still thought necessary to represent 'communities', though some counties were divided in order to diminish the expense of elections. Also, some weight was given to population in 1832, so that some single-member boroughs were created. On the other hand, the idea of giving representation according to population through single-member constituencies was not adopted until 1885, and even then not completely. The change then became possible and desirable because of the social development which I have already described. It was no longer conceivable that a huge city like Birmingham should have the same representation as, say, Bath or Blackpool. Therefore Birmingham had to be divided into several single-member constituencies, and the representation of each area was based on population. In other words, the principle of equality of representation, or 'one man, one vote, one value', had almost been accepted.

Even so, there were and still are exceptions. The population of England grows faster than that of Wales and Scotland, but it would obviously be undesirable gradually to reduce the proportionate representation of those countries. This principle might apply to the several parts of England if its population were not so homogeneous. On the other hand, Northern Ireland has less than proportionate

Democracy

representation because it has its own Parliament in Belfast. Also it is still not thought desirable to cut across county and borough boundaries. The city is a social unit, and if it is not large enough to have eight members it ought to have seven, not be divided so as to share a member with part of the neighbouring county. For these reasons the population of one constituency may be much larger than that of another, though independent commissions re-arrange constituencies on a basis of equality of representation at frequent intervals.

Thus, even the United Kingdom does not press the principle with ruthless logic. In any case it is really not a principle. It was found by experience that the single-member constituency, with something like equality of representation, suited British political and social conditions. Nobody would say that it was an essential element in democracy, and there are many varieties of representation in other parts of the Commonwealth.

Representative government

The House of Commons is now regarded as the representative House because its members are elected. There is still a House of Lords, and even a hundred years ago its members would have denied that they were unrepresentative. Apart from a few life peers (including judges) who have since been added, its members were in 1763 as they still are in 1963, bishops and hereditary peers, all of whom were (though in many cases they no longer are) great landowners. In what was called the 'well-ordered hierarchy' of the eighteenth century, when Great Britain was still primarily an agricultural country, representation was founded not on people as such but on land. Nor was this as absurd as it now seems to modern Englishmen. The villager was dependent on his squire; the interests of the squire were dependent on those of the great landowners like the Duke of Marlborough, the Duke of Bedford, or the Earl of Lonsdale. It was, therefore, very proper that the great landowners, including the bishops, should be hereditary legislators. Even the House of Commons consisted mainly of landowners, though it also contained merchants, lawyers and other representatives of the small but important urban middle class.

The development of industrialisation, as I have already explained, altered social conditions, and the relative position of the House of Lords gradually declined. The House of Commons became the 'representative' House as industry replaced land as the dominant factor and the typical Englishman became not a peasant or agricultural labourer but an industrial worker. Accordingly, when in the early years of the present century the House of Lords began to use its ancient powers a frontal attack was made upon them. In effect that House cannot now defeat any financial Bill, and it can delay it for not more than one month; nor can it defeat any other public Bill—except a Bill to extend the maximum period of a Parliament beyond five years—nor delay it for more than one year.

The composition of the House of Lords has not been substantially altered, not because anybody is now satisfied with it, but because general agreement about a new Second Chamber has not been attained. The British Constitution has adapted itself to a bicameral system, and the House of Lords does valuable and indeed essential work. Because it has been deprived of most of its powers, its debates can range widely and are not dominated by the party contest. Much valuable work is done in committee on public Bills, private Bills, and statutory orders. A substantial minority of its members still exhibit that strong sense of public duty which had become traditional with the peerage. Though nearly everybody thinks that the House of Lords ought to be reformed, there is equally wide agreement that some form of Second Chamber is needed, without affecting the ultimate responsibility of the House of Commons.

Responsible government

The Anglo-Norman system of representation was not peculiar to England, but its development into representative government, with effective power vested in the House of Commons, was due to the conflict between the Crown and Parliament in the seventeenth century. Executive power was retained by the King, who determined both the composition and the policy of his government. He and his government also had considerable power, through influence at elections, over the composition of the House of Commons. The American Declaration of Independence, 1776, was therefore an attack on the alleged 'tyrannies' of King George III; and the Constitution of the

Democracy

United States was carefully designed to prevent such 'tyrannies'. The executive powers were vested in an elected President, his political appointments had to be confirmed by the Senate, and none of his officials could sit in either House of the Congress. Hence the Americans have what is called a Presidential system, with a separation of powers which implies, among other things, a clear distinction between executive and legislative powers.

The evolution in Great Britain was quite different. Effective power was gradually transferred from the King to his Ministers, and those Ministers had to have the support of a majority in the House of Commons. This evolution was possible through the growth of parties, and the system works best where there are two major parties —though of course anybody can start a party if he can find people to follow his leadership.

There are, however, less obvious implications. The party is based upon leadership and policy, continuing from generation to generation. If it were based merely on political ambition or corruption, as the so-called 'parties' were in the eighteenth century (though there were other elements), its life would be essentially temporary. A mere collection of politicians, banded together by self-interest, will inevitably break up. The British parties, though of comparatively recent creation (the Conservative Party may be said to date from 1832, the Liberal Party from 1865, and the Labour Party from 1899), have deep roots because they represent persistent points of view. The Conservatives usually trace their descent from the Reformation of the sixteenth century, the Liberals from the conflicts of the seventeenth century, and the Labour Party from the peasants' revolt of the late fourteenth century. There is, of course, no continuity of organisation except from the nineteenth century, but it is essential to remember that parties are not mere groups of ambitious politicians, but upholders of principles of government. As such they develop a strong internal loyalty. To betray the party, whether the betrayal is done by the leaders or the followers, is not merely politically undesirable but also disloyal.

Moreover, it is not enough to have a party. It is necessary to persuade electors to support it. This is done partly by organisation in depth, so that every party has an active local organisation in nearly every one of the 630 constituencies, and partly by a continuous effort of political education, applying political principles to the problems of the day. This assumes, of course, an electorate which is politically speaking, already highly educated. The British are the world's greatest readers of newspapers; almost every home has a wireless set and most have television sets. The newspapers are usually partisan, but if they are too obviously partisan they will lose readers. The broadcasting and television authorities are required by law to be politically impartial. Political broadcasts, in the party sense, are provided by the parties, and are publicised as such, but all discussions of political and social problems affect the minds of the electors and help them to determine their votes. A British party has therefore to support policies which seem sensible to ordinary people who are accustomed to the maintenance of political argument at a high level. Elections are won not by electioneering, but by consistent behaviour which retains the loyalty and support of fifteen million electors who know the distinction between a politician and a statesman.

This analysis of the essentials of the British system of democratic government shows that it need not be, and indeed cannot be, copied in all its details. The establishment of a new democratic system is in any case something of a leap in the dark, but it is clearly undesirable to assume that African electors, or African politicians, will behave like British electors, or British politicians. They cannot, because their background and traditions are different. The anxiety of African politicians to build a new social order is commendable, but they cannot revolutionise popular ideas by constitutional reform; they have to build the one upon the other. It is not enough to copy rules, forms and ceremonies which are full of meaning to one people and mean nothing whatever to another. A process of adaptation to local circumstances is essential.

IV. *The Social Order*

Every society has a traditional social order. The nomadic tribes of Europe which eventually settled on the land and formed the modern nation-states had, we believe, very much the same sort of social order as is to be found in the few remaining nomadic tribes of Africa and Asia. The fundamental units of the social order were the family and the tribe. The European family was usually patriarchal, i.e. the grandfather was the head of the family, and to him his sons and his grandsons, their wives, and his daughters and grand-daughters, so long as they were unmarried, owed obedience and deference. When a daughter or a grand-daughter married she joined her husband's family. The property of the family—its tents, cattle, sheep and horses —were under the control of the grandfather. This system is called 'patriarchal' from the Latin word *pater*, which means 'father'. The other system, the 'matriarchal', which comes from the Latin word *mater* or 'mother', was more common in Asia than in Europe. In this case the husband joined the *wife's* family.

In either case a collection of families, large or small, formed the tribe, which usually had an elected or hereditary chief and either a tribal assembly or a council of elders (or both) whose decisions the members of the tribe respected. The whole tribe was governed by a system of tribal, or customary, law which every member of the tribe recognised to be binding upon him. Nor did the system change when the tribe settled on the land. The tribal law became more complicated because rights in land can be much more complicated than rights in cattle. Land law is highly complex law.

The long-term effect of settlement was, however, to replace the tribal system by a more complicated system of government. The tribal law became local customary law, and to it were added various types of legislation. The foundation of the social order is nevertheless essentially the same whether it derives from tribal law, local customary law, or a modern written constitution. It is a recognition by the individual of his obligations to his fellow-men and his rulers in accordance with the laws and social conventions for the time being recognised. It involves mutual recognition of property rights, the mutual obligations of husbands and wives and of parents and children, the obligation to allow other men to go about their lawful business without interference, the obligations arising out of agreements, and so forth. Breaches of these obligations are not uncommon, whether in a tribal or in a highly complex settled society. They may take two forms, breaches by individuals who think that they can improve their positions by breaking their social obligations, and breaches by organised bodies of men who seek to subvert social institutions and perhaps to replace them.

The former cause no great difficulty in a well-ordered society because that society is organised to deal with such anti-social action. The maintenance of law and order is one of the essential functions of government. In tribal societies the chief and the elders try to settle disputes by peaceful means and call on the tribe to help put down breaches of the social order where peaceful means prove unsuccessful. In more complex societies there are law courts, police forces and, in the last resort, the armed forces. The efficacy of these methods depends on the general observance of the law at all social levels. Let me illustrate by taking the example of England once more.

My College was founded in Cambridge in 1350 by a bishop who secured the permission of the Archbishop of Canterbury and King Edward III. It was therefore lawfully established as a charitable or religious foundation. For more than six hundred years its Masters, Fellows and members have, almost invariably, observed the terms of the foundation. Whenever the office of Master is vacant the Fellows elect a Master in accordance with the law; the Master observes the statutes and recognises the authority of the Governing Body; the members recognise the authority of the Governing Body and the Master. All these obligations can be enforced in accordance with the law of England; but in the course of six hundred years this has rarely been necessary, and not at all for the last two hundred years. We are responsible people doing our best to carry out the purposes of the foundation to which we have been elected. No force is needed to

The Social Order

persuade us to do our duty. It would, however, be impossible for the College to carry on if Cambridge were not a peaceful and well-ordered city, in which the College can retain its property, make contracts for the repair of its buildings and the purchase of stores, obtain gas, electricity and water, empty its drains into public sewers, be secure against epidemics, cash its cheques, exchange services for notes and coins, exchange notes and coins for goods and services, employ servants, and so forth. When I leave my home in the College to walk to my bank, I assume, as a matter of course, that in my absence my family and my property will be safe. I do not take any kind of weapon with me because I believe that I shall be unmolested. I keep to the pavement when I can, because I believe that the motor traffic will keep to the road. When I have to cross the road I assume that the motor traffic will observe the rules of the road. At the bank I assume that my account is in credit because I assume that the Bursar of the College has paid my salary. I accept currency notes in exchange for my cheque because I believe that the shopkeepers of Cambridge will accept notes in exchange for the goods which I require and that my servants will accept notes in exchange for their services.

Here is a collection of beliefs or assumptions, and yet I have only taken a walk to my bank. At any given moment fifty million people in Britain are making assumptions about the behaviour of fifty million people. They believe that almost everybody will obey the law.

Not only are there rules which people normally obey. There are also rules of behaviour in case people do not. If somebody broke into my house during my absence, my wife would at once telephone the nearest police station. She would assume that there was somebody on duty both at the telephone exchange and at the police station. The sergeant at the police station would at once send a couple of men to the house. They would assume that every citizen would help to apprehend the housebreaker; that if they found him they could keep him in the station for not more twenty-four hours; that a magistrate would be ready to receive the charge at any time; and that the legal system would be put in motion. In other words, there is a system of law enforcement which depends on the assumption that private citizens, police officers, prison officers, magistrates and judges would themselves apply the law. If, on the other hand, the wrong

Democracy in Africa

which I alleged was not criminal, but, let us say, my path to the bank was obstructed, or the bank failed to cash my cheque on demand, I should instruct my solicitor to take legal proceedings; he and I would make another series of assumptions about the behaviour of the officers and judges of the law courts.

It is thus plain that social life in England depends upon the belief or confidence of Englishmen in the general observance of the law of England. That confidence is seldom misplaced. Some Englishmen do break the law, but they are a small minority and can easily be dealt with by the organs of government maintained for that purpose, and with the active assistance of private citizens. They will be dealt with by the judges and the magistrates, the police officers and the prison officers, so as to ensure that the law is applied and enforced 'freely and fairly, without favour and without fear'. What is more, we can assume that any lawful authority will be accepted by nearly everybody. The Governing Body of my College, the authorities of the City of Cambridge, the Ministers and the civil servants, the judges and the magistrates, the police and the armed forces must keep within their powers; but when they are acting within their powers their orders will almost invariably be obeyed. Before going into battle against the French fleet Admiral Lord Nelson hoisted the signal, 'England expects that every man this day will do his duty'. That principle applies not merely to the officers and men of the Royal Navy on a particular occasion. It applies to all public servants and all citizens at all times. It is assumed as a matter of course that every public servant will do his duty honestly and efficiently, whether it be pleasant or unpleasant, and without nepotism or corruption. If he does not he ought to be, and is, dismissed from his post, whether he be Lord Chancellor or a porter. But the ordinary citizen cannot expect public servants to do their duty unless he himself does his duty, as citizen, as Master of a College, as secretary to a football club, as trade union official, as schoolmaster, as driver of a motor car, as Moderator of the Church of Scotland, as householder, as father of a family, as shopkeeper, as employer of labour, or as plain citizen.

It is necessary to emphasise not merely the hierarchy of government but also the economic order. The cultivator sows his land because he thinks he will be able to reap his crop; the owner of cattle feeds them

The Social Order

because he thinks he will be able to use or sell their produce; the shopkeeper buys goods because he thinks he will be able to sell them; the industrialist sets up machinery, buys raw materials and employs men because he thinks he will be able to sell the finished articles; the employee works because he thinks he will be paid for his service; the capitalist lends money because he thinks he will be paid interest and, in due course, will be repaid his loan. Everybody uses banks, cheques and money because everybody has confidence in them. A man is even prepared to make annual payments to an insurance company because he believes that, after his death, the company will make annual payments to his widow. In short, the economic order, like the rest of the social order, depends on confidence. Everybody believes that everybody else will do his duty according to law. Indeed, there is more to it than that. The children, the aged, the cripples, the blind, the deaf, the dumb and everybody else under disability have to be maintained by somebody, and it is not enough for every man to do his duty; he must do more out of charity or compassion. In a highly regulated state like that of Great Britain much is done by public services; but there are also religious and charitable foundations, colleges and schools, hospitals and homes for the aged, orphanages and youth hostels and so forth, all maintained by endowments from benefactors. There is a host of societies, maintained by endowments, donations and subscriptions, for the public good, perhaps to purchase works of art for the public art galleries, perhaps to help in the preservation of historic buildings, perhaps to further the study of international relations, perhaps to provide financial assistance to students, perhaps to help refugees from tyranny. It is essential to a well-ordered community not only that everybody should have confidence in everybody else but also that there should be a substantial supply of persons ready to contribute money and service to good causes.

What has been said about England could be said, with some variations of detail, about every well-ordered democratic society. Englishmen are not by nature any more law-abiding than anybody else. They and their ancestors have, however, much experience of war, civil war, riots, strikes, financial crises, nepotism, corruption, religious persecution, and indeed almost all the ills to which a community can be subjected. They have done their best to get rid of them because they know from their own experience as well as from the experience of others that, whoever gains by them, the mass of the people suffer.

The social order thus depends on the confidence of ordinary citizens in the behaviour of other people. This is so whatever the nature of the society or the form of government. The modern commercial or industrial society is, however, much more complicated and therefore much more fragile than a system based upon peasant cultivation. The peasant may suffer from drought or flood or locusts or cattle disease or tribal warfare; but, these hazards excepted, he expects to reap where he has sown and to be able to take the produce from his cattle, sheep or goats. In the great cities, however, hardly anybody produces anything for himself. His livelihood depends on other people behaving as he expects them to behave. If, for instance, confidence in the currency is lost, everybody will rush to convert currency notes and bank deposits into durable articles, and the machinery of trade and employment will break down. If employers fear that they will be unable to sell, production will be stopped and there will be mass unemployment. Even law and order may break down, by a strike of the police, or by large-scale rioting, or by a running down of the efficiency of government. Such difficulties have occurred in Europe in recent times, but they happen even more easily in educationally less-developed countries, or in countries with insufficient or inefficient communications, because it is less easy to dispel rumours and reassure the population. In fact, the confidence on which the social order depends is in large measure a compound of social tradition and efficient government.

The efficiency does not depend only on ability to call out armed forces, though that is essential. The armed forces themselves obey orders because they have a traditional discipline and because they accept the orders of the government. It depends also on making certain that law-breakers will be dealt with. Much depends on the discipline and morale of the police, whose efficiency may be undermined by political corruption, or by the reluctance of politicians to give the necessary orders, or by corruption or inefficiency in the judicial machine. Examples could be quoted in which the efficiency of the police has gradually run down and anarchy spread widely. The

The Social Order

situation is particularly dangerous where there is an active communist party whose essential function is to create chaos in order to provide an opportunity for the 'dictatorship of the proletariat'—which means dictatorship by communist leaders. They rely for this purpose on the tradition of democratic free speech, which of course they abolish as soon as they achieve power, and on a variety of slogans depending on popular prejudices, which they adopt for purely tactical reasons.

Much depends, finally, on the attitude of the people themselves. Any substantial section can without great difficulty create chaos if they so desire and have an efficient organisation. No police force can deal with a considerable number of incidents arising in different places at the same time. It has to rely on help from members of the public. The task of statesmanship is to produce a nice combination of persuasion and force, persuasion of the law-abiding citizens and force against those who are potential law-breakers. This requires experience which few African politicians can hope to possess until they have been in office for some years.

Every schoolboy knows that he can balance a stick on his fingers so long as he moves his hand in the direction in which it is tending to fall. If somebody gives his hand a jerk, or if he takes his eyes off the stick, the stick will come crashing to the ground. So it is with the social order. So long as we all believe in the stability of the social order we sleep peacefully in our beds at night, leave our homes next morning to go to our jobs, go home in the evening expecting to find meals waiting for us, go along to the beer hall or the cinema or watch television, and go to bed believing, in the popular phrase, that 'tomorrow is another day', i.e. that we can repeat the experience tomorrow. But if the social order breaks down we have to stay up all night to keep off intruders, we cannot go to our jobs because there are none, there are no meals because we can earn no money, if we have money we discover that nobody wants those coins or pieces of paper, the beer halls and the cinemas are closed, and anyhow we cannot go to them because somebody might hit us over the head or shoot us down from a veranda—all, perhaps, because a set of rowdy schoolboys has not been spanked, or because some demagogue has been making inflammatory speeches and a number of people have been silly enough to listen to him, or because some people have real grievances and try to find a quick solution to them.

Let it be emphasized that these propositions apply to all sorts of people in all sorts of societies. The examples differ from society to society. Government depends essentially on confidence in the social order being maintained, and this depends on the general observance of laws and conventions, by the rulers as by the ruled. One cannot break some laws and conventions and expect other laws and conventions to be observed.

V. Change in Africa

'Africa', it is said, 'is on the march'. This is a way of saying that, almost everywhere in Africa, traditional ideas are being given up and replaced by ideas imported from Western culture. We have seen how, in countries like England and France, the comparatively simple ideas of the Germanic tribes were developed into the complex ideas of the modern nationalist states. In most parts of Africa comparable changes are taking place, but in a generation or two, not in a thousand years. The question is often asked, how quickly these changes can be effected. There is no simple answer to that question because it depends on what people want, how competent individuals are, and what risks people are prepared to run.

What people want is usually put into some simple formula like 'freedom from colonial rule', but that formula is inadequate because freedom from colonial rule might mean anarchy, and nobody wants that. It might also mean a return to the tribal system which operated before the Arab and European intrusions. In some parts of Africa, where the infiltration of Western ideas has been small, that might still be practicable. Elsewhere it is impracticable because colonial rule has changed the environment too much. Western medicine and new methods of production have allowed the population to grow and have found means for maintaining it by the production of cash crops like cocoa, coffee, bananas, oil seeds, tea, cotton, sisal and so on, or by improved cattle production, or by mining gold, uranium, copper, tin, aluminium or coal, or by the establishment of secondary industries, or by exploiting the timber resources of the jungle. In the process great towns have been established and there has been a large infusion of European or Asian enterprise which no one could remove, even if this were considered just, without disrupting the African economy. The statement that a return to tribalism is impracticable does not, however, necessarily imply that the remains of the tribes must be eliminated. It is possible to fit the tribes into some other form of government; and if loyalty to chiefs is still an element in the local environment it should be done.

In most parts of Africa there has been, moreover, a development of nationalist ideas. A small English-educated (or French-educated) minority has been created, and its principal demand is for self-government. There are ambiguities in this phrase, and they are not always made clear. In the 'Crown Colony' system of government which applied to most of the British territories in Africa, the local responsibility for government was vested in the Governor. His policies required the approval of a Secretary of State in London, and the Secretary of State was responsible to the Parliament of the United Kingdom. Nationalist propaganda tends to minimise the advantages of this system and to exaggerate its disadvantages. Political propaganda, whether in Europe or in Africa, must always be regarded with some suspicion because behind it is inevitably a mixture of motives. A Colonial Governor is invariably anxious for the peace and prosperity of the inhabitants of the colony or protectorate. On the other hand, he is also a careerist. Like the Master of a College he wants to make a success of his job. His success depends mainly on the peace and prosperity of the colony or protectorate. One assumes, therefore, that in his reports and despatches to the Secretary of State, in his speeches, and in other local propaganda, he tends to make himself appear more successful than he actually is.

That assumption will probably be accepted by everybody, but it applies even more strongly to politicians, whether they are European, Asian or African. However public-spirited they may be, and they usually are, they have also a pretty obvious streak of personal ambition. What is more, since the task of the politician is to place himself in power, he necessarily magnifies not only his own merits but also the defects of those already in power. This applies in Britain as elsewhere. The politicians in power praise their achievements; the politicians not in power deny that there have been any achievements worth praising but assert that there will be achievements when the politicians in power are turned out and those out of power come in. We in Britain are, however, used to alternations of power and therefore take all political propaganda with some scepticism. The government

Change in Africa

is neither as good as it pretends to be nor as bad as the opposition claims it to be. Under colonial rule, on the other hand, the colonial politicians have had no experience by which the strength or weakness of their propaganda can be judged. They are an opposition which has never become a government, and therefore they can attack all along the line without being asked the devastating question: what did you do better when *you* were in office. Just as I have never seen any opposition propaganda in Britain that was not exaggerated, so I have never seen any anti-colonial propaganda in Asia or in Africa that was not exaggerated.

The substitution of an African Government for a Colonial Government will in fact have no effect whatever if the two are equally efficient and follow the same policy. The man in the town or the village will be precisely where he was. Leaving aside the question of efficiency, to which we must return, there are, however, two possibilities. First, the African Government may change the policy. The anti-colonial politicans in fact always attack the colonial policy and promise to substitute a new one. That new policy cannot be evaluated in the abstract, because its value depends upon a just appreciation of its content. When the inevitable exaggerations have been cut away, will it be a better policy from the point of view of all the people, or of some of them? If it is a better policy from the point of view of some, but a worse from the point of view of others, how do the advantages and the disadvantages come out in the balance? Even if everybody were free of prejudice it would not be easy to answer these questions. In fact, however, nearly all the people who judge, including the African politicians as well as the British, are thoroughly prejudiced.

The second possibility is, I think, more important. A system of government can never be really successful unless it has the active support of the people who are being governed, or at least of a substantial portion of them. That can happen under the colonial system. It certainly happened in most of the British colonial territories early in the present century, and it seems still to be so in some of them—Hong Kong is the obvious example because it has provided a refuge for so many of those who, very wisely, prefer colonial rule to communist rule. As colonial nationalism has developed, however, the number of territories in which the colonial people have been satisfied with colonial rule has rapidly diminished. It is true that the number of active nationalists is small; they are to be found mainly among the English-educated. Generally, however, they are able to obtain increasing support among the ordinary people. Much of that support may be derived from misleading propaganda. This is dangerous in the long run, because the ordinary people will expect from self-government or independence advantages that they will not in fact get. The reaction cannot set in, however, until self-government or independence has been attained. If self-government or independence is held up, therefore, the process of government becomes increasingly difficult, and the British Government has to consider whether it is not better to confer self-government quickly rather than to contemplate a slow run-down in the process of government.

The reasons which at first inclined the British Government to believe that progress towards self-government ought to be slow will appear presently. The essential reason for changing that belief was that colonial politicians were not prepared to agree to such slow progress. Their fundamental belief—and it really is a belief, not a mere cloak for their own ambitions—is that self-government is both just and desirable. They consider it to be just because they accept the nationalist thesis that national self-government is the ultimate good; every nation, they believe, has a right to govern itself; to be governed by British officials, acting under the control of British politicians, is contrary to the national dignity. Good government, in the time-honoured phrase, is no substitute for self-government. They also believe—and here again they are usually honest in their belief, though they are more likely to have been convinced by their own arguments than by the facts on which those arguments ought to be based—that their policy will be better for the people at large than the policy followed by British Governments. They assume, usually but not always erroneously, that British Governments are concerned more with the interests of the British people than with the interests of the colonial people.

Once these opinions become widespread the task of colonial government becomes increasingly difficult. Political agitation, in countries which are not used to it, usually leads to violence. The colonial politicians necessarily appeal for popular support, and they

Change in Africa

have to exaggerate their case. Even when there is no rioting or sabotage against the colonial government there are likely to be disputes among the communal groups. Colonial territories are not inhabited by homogeneous peoples. It is an exercise in nationalist fiction to assume that, say, Nigeria is inhabited by persons who think of themselves as Nigerians, or Ceylon by persons who think of themselves as Ceylonese. Political education has not proceeded so far; and most people think of themselves as Yoruba or Ibo, Sinhalese or Tamil. If there is a prospect of British rule ending there at once arises a competition for power, a competition between politicians who have communal support.

Experience in India between 1937 and 1947 had a profound effect on British policy. Self-government for India had been proclaimed as British policy, by authority of the British Parliament, as early as 1919. It was thought that the transition would have to be slow, but it was too slow for the Indian politicians. The Indian National Congress was organised in depth and it had the leadership of Mahatma Gandhi. Gandhi had strong religious objection to violence and therefore, when argument proved unconvincing, he advocated a policy of non-violent non-co-operation. Whenever he called for non-violence, however, violence was the consequence because the Indians were not all Gandhis, and some of them were communists who wanted to exploit nationalist sentiment in order to create chaos. The Muslims took fright at the possibility of a Hindu-dominated government and most of them became equally strongly organised in the Muslim League. At the level of the 'high commands' the Hindu-Muslim conflict was an oratorical contest; at the level of the village it was often a riot. Both sides, of course, blamed the British; but that is a regular feature of nationalist propaganda. From 1940 the British were in fact trying to find a solution acceptable to both sides. In the end they forced a solution by threatening to walk out. In fact, they did walk out too quickly, though by agreement with the Indian and Pakistani leaders; and they must bear some share of responsibility for the riots which preceded and followed the transfer of power.

Where a colonial power really intends to continue to rule it has no great difficulty in putting down nationalist movements, as the Spaniards and the Portuguese have demonstrated in Africa. Britain has no such intention and British public opinion finds it as distasteful to have to use force against nationalist agitators, in defence of law and order, as it would to use force against political opponents in the United Kingdom. British policy has, therefore, recognised that the process of conferring self-government must be accelerated. An attempt is made to make the transfer gradual, but 'gradualness' is a matter of degree, and it is recognised that the lengthy periods adopted in India and Ceylon are no longer practicable. This means that risks must be taken; and a consideration of those risks brings us back to efficiency.

A British Government is chosen from 630 members of Parliament and some 900 members of the House of Lords. The 630 members of Parliament are selected by active party organisations because their views are likely to be approved by a majority of literate and quite reasonably educated electors. Most junior Ministers have been Members of Parliament for at least four years. Most Cabinet Ministers have had considerable experience as Junior Ministers. A Prime Minister usually has lengthy Cabinet experience as well as much experience in office. Where these conditions do not operate, as with the Labour Government of 1924, mistakes are almost certain to be made. These conditions cannot be produced in newly-independent countries, though it is always hoped to provide at least a few years of Ministerial office for those who are likely to assume power. The most favourable conditions were those in Ceylon in 1947; the Prime Minister had held office for 16 years and several others had been in office for 11 years. The first Cabinet was by no means as efficient as a British Cabinet, but it was quite reasonably efficient. Also, leadership of a nationalist movement, especially one organised in depth like the Indian National Congress, is itself a qualification. Politicians in opposition, as nationalist politicians almost always are, tend to believe in their own exaggerations, but at least they learn to formulate their political ideas, and sometimes they learn from the mistakes of others, if not from their own. What is more, nationalist politics tend to throw up persons of unusual merit. Jahawarlal Nehru was an obvious leader; but D. S. Senanayake in Ceylon and Tunku Abdul Rahman in Malaya were not, and they surprised everybody who knew them. One has to be wary of megalomaniacs or pocket Hitlers;

Change in Africa

there is also a risk of political careerists, sometimes corrupt, joining the winning side—there have been some obvious examples in Asia. Nevertheless, it is rarely difficult to find political leaders who can assume the responsibility for government immediately after the termination of British rule, provided that they are given a reasonable transitional experience. This has been shown in Ghana, Nigeria, Sierra Leone, Tanganyika, the Federation of Malaya and Singapore, Jamaica, Trinidad, Cyprus and Uganda. It was one of the discoveries of the fifties.

Political leaders do not govern, however; their task is to direct government, to determine its policy. The process of government requires an efficient civil service—which in the British sense includes all civilian administrators and technicians—an efficient and disciplined police force and, if there is any risk of rioting, a trained and disciplined army. Ideally these should be staffed by local people, since Ministers often suspect—usually quite unnecessarily— the *bona fides* of British officers who have been used to a colonial régime. On the other hand, an efficient machine cannot be built up in less than two generations, particularly in the military services, the law and the technical services in which long experience is required. There was no great difficulty in India, because the Indian Civil Service and most of the legal and technical services had been reasonably Indianised. The armed forces had few Indian officers of high rank, but most Indian officers had had experience either of war or of civil disturbance, and some had both. Moreover, if there is a sufficiency of junior officers and non-commissioned officers, it is possible to borrow a few senior officers from the British armed forces, as India, Pakistan, Ceylon and Ghana have done. It is not so easy to borrow civilian officials or technical officers because Britain has no surplus, though the recent decision by the United Kingdom Government to bear a substantial part of the cost of overseas officers in the service of governments before and after independence—if those governments so choose— may make it easier.

Pakistan had much greater difficulty than India because comparatively few of the senior officials in undivided India had been Muslims, and some of the best of those who were decided to remain in India. Pakistan had one senior official of the highest ability, Chaudhri Mohamed Ali, afterwards Prime Minister. He did a most efficient job of organisation in 1947, but he had to use what personnel was available, and some of it was of poor quality. A few British officials were offered careers in the Pakistan services and, with the comparatively few Pakistani officials of long experience, they were able to establish a reasonably efficient administration. There were, however, defects of administration which were among the reasons alleged for the suspension of the constitution by General Ayub Khan in 1959. On the other hand, Pakistan had had a high proportion of the officers of the Indian armed forces, and was therefore able to build up very efficient forces with the assistance of a few seconded British officers. Even so, the steps necessary to provide separate Indian and Pakistani police and armed forces had not been taken before the 15th August 1947. Everybody, including the Governor-General and the Indian and Pakistani leaders, was too impatient. Another six months might have made a great deal of difference on the new frontiers and would not only have prevented many murders and abductions, but also would have given millions of refugees confidence in the new administration. There would probably have been a seepage of refugees both ways, but not the mass movements which were produced by loss of confidence.

In Ceylon, too, most of the civil services had been Ceylonised before independence, though there was a shortage of senior civil servants of ability and also an acute shortage of technical officers. Attempts were made, usually successfully, to retain the services of the best of the European officers, who had in any case been used to working with Ceylonese Ministers between 1931 and 1947. Small armed forces had been built up since 1931, and there were Ceylonese officers both in the navy and in the army. With some assistance from the United Kingdom these services were expanded, though British troops remained in the island, by agreement, until 1956. On the other hand, Burma suffered severely from administrative and technical inefficiency. Until 1937 Burma was administered as part of India, but there were few Burmese in the Indian services. From 1942 to 1945 Burma was occupied by the Japanese, and few Burmese obtained any experience of any value. Nevertheless, the Burmese Ministers decided for independence outside the Commonwealth in 1947. They were able to obtain few experienced officials and technicians, whether from the United Kingdom or from India. Civil war broke out, and there have been Chinese troops on Burman territory. The Burman officials have learned their jobs the hard way. Burma is still the least efficient of the territories which were formerly British, but there are even worse administered territories in Asia.

The examples of India, Pakistan and Ceylon could not be followed in West Africa because the process of Africanisation would have taken too long. It was possible to have only short periods of transition from full colonial status to full self-government. It was therefore necessary to do two things. First, it was necessary to appoint comparatively young and inexperienced officers to quite senior posts. There are serious risks in this process, but they are not unreasonable risks. A young officer who is intelligent, honest, hard-working, keen and ambitious is quite likely to take the measure of his unexpected and unusual responsibilities; what he probably lacks most is the undefinable quality called 'judgment'. It is founded on a varied experience but is of such a nature that there is an almost intuitive reaction to a new situation, which enables the official concerned to decide what is the right action to take. So long as the machinery of government works normally inexperienced Ministers and inexperienced officials together can run it without difficulty; the unusual or the unexpected is apt to produce hasty and ill-considered decisions.

The solution is to retain a sufficient number of experienced British officers. This is not always as easy as it sounds. Any successful British official or technical officer has a loyalty to the people whom he serves—if he has not he is not likely to be successful—but he has also to consider his career. If he is 35 years of age, and still more if he is 40 years of age, and he is merely being employed as a stop-gap until an African is thought to be ready to take over his job, he probably will not stay; every year of service in the country concerned, while increasing his value in that country, probably decreases his value elsewhere. In certain fields of activity, especially science and engineering, there is at present a shortage of experienced men, and high salaries are need to keep such men if they have no security of tenure. What is more, these officials are being asked to take serious political risks. They have no idea what the political situation may be in ten years' time, and therefore whether conditions will be such that their service is likely to continue.

Nor are these the only difficulties. The relations between Ministers and officials in the United Kingdom are governed by long tradition, and both the Ministers and the officials know where they stand in relation to each other. In a newly independent country this tradition has yet to be established. The situation is complicated by the fact that the officials had been the instruments of a colonial government while the Ministers have almost invariably been nationalist politicians in opposition not merely to the government but to officialdom generally. The Minister who was yesterday a 'rabble-rousing agitator', perhaps newly released from internment, and an official who was yesterday a 'lackey of imperialism' must today work together in intimate harmony to build a new nation. This is another reason for having a short transition. Its purpose is not merely to give the Minister experience of government but also to give the official experience of responsible government. If both are sensible people, particularly if both have a sense of humour, they will adapt themselves to each other.

These are not fundamental difficulties. The conditions on which colonial officials may be employed after independence are usually negotiated by the Colonial Office and the Ministers in the transition before independence. It must be confessed that hitherto the Colonial Office has been more successful in negotiating attractive terms for retirement than in providing terms which will encourage officials to stay; but as a result of a considerable number of recent experiments a good deal of experience has been gained; and, if nationalist politicians realise the difficulties inherent in rapid progress towards independence, it ought not to be difficult, under the new arrangements for the Overseas Service, to reach an agreement which satisfies both Ministers and officials.

The greater difficulties come after independence. Nationalist politicians rarely think in economic terms, except in so far as they give the impression in their speeches that economic conditions will inevitably improve after independence. This is almost invariably the impression that the people receive from the propaganda; and they are thinking not in the long term but in the short term. That is to say, they assume that, immediately after independence, the ordinary African will be better off than he was before independence. It is extremely unlikely that he will be, but if he lives in a city he will notice

Change in Africa

that some others are—that the politicians have large cars and substantial salaries, that a number of English-speaking officials have received promotion, that a number of new jobs has been created—for instance in the diplomatic service and the armed forces—for favoured persons, and that quite a number of people are given free trips to London, New York, and other far-off places. The truth is, of course, that independence benefits immediately only the members of the educated middle class, and perhaps not all of them. The ordinary man may be gratified to see that, whereas before independence only the Governor had a flag on his car, now all the Ministers have flags on their cars. He may be happy to see that the same old bus or truck, on which he has to travel, is now brightened by the new national flag, but it does not appear to improve the comfort of the journey. We must come back to this point because nationalist politicians and the new officials do not always realise that their new dignities have a different look to those who do not share in them.

If the transition to independence is well prepared, there ought not to be any serious economic consequences immediately. It must, however, be appreciated that the economy depends on confidence, on the stability of the currency, the belief by sellers that they will get paid, the belief of purchasers that goods will be delivered, the belief of producers that they will continue to have markets, the belief of employees that they will get their wages, the belief of investors that they will get dividends, and so on. If the transition is not well-prepared, there is a risk of a run on the banks, a flight from the currency, a breakdown of commercial credit, and so forth; and this may cause the shops to shut, employers to stand off their employees, and capitalists to repatriate their capital. These things can happen even in the most stable economies, and the economy of a country is not stable if politically the country is unstable. Of the consequences to the social order of a breakdown of confidence I have already said something in chapter IV. If the nationalist politicians have the support of the mass of the people it ought not to happen, though even then the transition must be prepared with some care, so that everybody becomes used to the idea that there will be a new political order, without any change in the social order, on 'Independence Day'.

It cannot be assumed, however, that everybody will be prepared for majority rule on Independence Day, because majority rule may mean communal rule. The Muslims of India believed in 1947 that the Hindu majority would oppress them. The Hindus had no intention of doing so, as the event showed, but no time was allowed for the edge to be taken off the Hindu-Muslim conflict. In Ceylon the creation of a Pan-Sinhalese Ministry—from which the Tamils and the Muslims were excluded—in 1935 was a grievous error; but from 1942 D. S. Senanayake set himself to repair the error and the government of 1947, which achieved independence in 1948, had Tamil and Muslim members. In Malaya, the United Malay Nationalist Organisation secured the agreement of the Malayan Chinese Association and the Malayan Indian Congress. Even in Ghana Dr Nkrumah compromised with the Ashanti, though the compromise did not last very long. In Nigeria great care was taken over several years to secure general agreement with the terms of the constitution eventually adopted. These are the examples to be followed, not those of Burma, Indonesia and the Congo, where the first task of the partisan politicians was to do battle with other partisan politicians.

It is in the longer term that the problems arise, and they are of many kinds. The Indian National Congress has kept together under the leadership of Jawaharlal Nehru. Bold measures for the improvement of the Indian economy have been taken. They would have failed but for financial support from other countries and it is still not certain that they will succeed. Meanwhile, there have been in the states an excess of 'party politics', based mainly on the petty ambitions of minor politicians, a good deal of local corruption, and some disorder stimulated mainly by communist activity. It is not suggested that India would have been better off under British rule. On the contrary, the Indian Government has faced its difficulties nobly. All that is suggested is that the process of government is much more difficult than it appears to be in pre-independence nationalist propaganda. The substitution of one form of government for another form of government does not in itself solve economic and social problems, though it may make them easier to tackle.

The creation of Pakistan as a home for the Muslims of India provided an incentive which carried the country through the enormous difficulties of the transition. The death of Mohamed Ali Jinnah in 1948 and the murder of his principal lieutenant, Liaqat Ali Khan, in 1951, in effect broke up the Muslim League. The murder of Liaqat was symbolic. A state can be founded on religion if the people are agreed both on theology and on its social implications. Liaqat was a 'liberal' Muslim whose wife was a Christian. His assassin had a firm belief in the traditional social order of Islam. The assassination was an isolated phenomenon, not part of a political conspiracy. The riots in the Punjab in 1952 were, however, due to a conflict between orthodox Muslims and the rich and powerful Ahmadiya sect. Khwaja Nazimuddin's Government, as Chief Justice Munir showed afterwards in a remarkable report, felt itself unable to take firm action against the orthodox Muslims who were the aggressors and the Governor-General dismissed it. Though Nazimuddin himself went into dignified retirement, his supporters in effect became a dissident faction of the Muslim League. Though for a time Chaudhri Mohamed Ali stopped the rot, he was a first-class administrator, not a politician, and he could not deal either with the intrigues in West Pakistan or with the tortuous and sometimes turbulent politics of East Pakistan. There was a gradual deterioration in the political situation, accompanied by accusations of corruption against some (though by no means all) of the leading politicians. Pakistan's experiment with democracy ended in 1959 with the military *coup d'état* of General Ayub Khan, the Commander-in-Chief. Here the problem was political, not economic, though the corruption was due in part to the restrictions on imports which became necessary when the prices of Pakistan's exports—mainly jute and cotton—dropped after the Korean War. The internal prices of imported articles rose, so that large profits could be made from smuggling or from import licences.

For Africa, Ceylon supplies the most relevant lessons. The transition to independence was long—perhaps too long—and no difficulties whatever arose in 1948. D. S. Senanayake had formed a strong government in 1947 and the United National Party, which he led, had almost unanimous backing. There was only one obvious source of danger. It was the nationalist propaganda which had preceded independence; for it gave the impression that there would be a great improvement in social and economic conditions as soon as the Ceylonese had power in their hands. It was of course obvious to detached observers that there would be no such miraculous change. The island would still be dependent on its exports of tea, rubber and coconut products. Though an agreement had been made for the United Kingdom Government, at the request of the Ceylon Government, to bear part of the responsibility for diplomatic representation and defence, there would necessarily be increased expenditure on governmental services, because some of the cost had hitherto fallen on United Kingdom funds. Hence there could be no immediate change except for the favoured few, the politicians themselves (or at least those who were not already rich men, as several of them were), and the educated young men who obtained good jobs. It is true that there was an increase of Government expenditure, but the most obvious beneficiaries—not the most numerous—were the young graduates who were able to drive about in the cars which they had obtained on easy terms because they had government jobs.

The consequences did not appear immediately. After the death of D. S. Senanayake in 1952 the United National Party, now led by his son, obtained a large majority. Opposition to it was nevertheless growing, led partly by the communists and partly by S. W. R. D. Bandaranaike, who had been virtually dismissed from the Government before D. S. Senanayake's death. Mr Bandaranaike's technique was to appeal to the communal sentiments of the Sinhalese and at the same time enter into electoral agreements with the communists. These apparently irreconcilable objects could be achieved because of the growing popular dislike of the United National Party. The man in the village, who had expected so much from independence, found that he had gained nothing whatever, unless it was a sense of satisfaction that the British officials had been replaced by Ceylonese Ministers. D. S. Senanayake, though a comparatively rich man, was at heart a villager. His son Dudley, though Cambridge-educated, carried his father's prestige for the year during which he was Prime Minister. Dudley's successor, Sir John Kotelawala, was a bluff and hearty landowner with many good qualities, but his heart was in Europe, not in the village. The combination of personal antagonism to some of the members of the United National Party, the realisation that, after all, independence did not benefit the ordinary man, the appeals to communal and religious (Buddhist) sentiment by Bandaranaike and his allies among the Buddhist priests, and the organisation of the trade unions by communist leaders, led to an anti-United National Party majority in 1956. From that point there was a gradual deterioration in public order and in the efficiency of government until, in 1958, a large part of the country was virtually controlled by the mob.

It has been suggested that the mistake in Ceylon was to adopt adult franchise. On the other hand, that franchise had been in operation since 1931, and until 1956 it had not been used particularly unwisely. There was some corruption and personation in the towns, and the quality of the average member was not high; but there have been worse elections in England than the Ceylon elections of 1947 and 1952. Three factors have to be emphasised. First, the pre-independence nationalist propaganda gave the impression that there would be an improvement of economic conditions after independence, though the economy of the island made such an impression unjustified. Secondly, the nationalist politicians and their advisers were misled by the evident nationalism of the English-educated class. Among the rest of the population nationalism was far less strong than communalism, which had active propagandists among the Buddhist priests. Ambitious politicians among the Sinhalese were able to capitalise this communal sentiment and thus to set up a communal reaction among the Tamils. Thirdly, nationalist politicians had even before independence been agitating for the substitution of the 'mother tongue' for English as official language and medium of instruction. This phrase 'mother tongue' induced a strange mood of self-deception. It seemed to put the local language into competition with English; there were, however, two local languages, Sinhalese and Tamil, which inevitably came into conflict as the competition with English was removed. The Sinhalese thought of the 'mother tongue' as Sinhalese, while the Tamils thought of it as Tamil. The *nationalist* agitation for 'mother tongue' therefore encouraged the *communal* demands for Sinhalese and for Tamil, and though for a time it was suggested that both might be used—nobody had the courage to work it out in detail—eventually it became clear to the Tamils that 'mother tongue' meant 'Sinhalese only'. Since 1956 Ceylon politics have been essentially communal, with the Tamils putting themselves up for auction and neither of the Sinhalese parties being willing to pay a high price because they would probably lose two Sinhalese seats for every Tamil seat that they purchased. Meanwhile there has been a gradual deterioration in the economic position of the island.

The examples of India, Pakistan and Ceylon are useful because there alone has there been some years' experience of the problems of self-government. The examples do not show the consequences of one possible line of development, that of a limited franchise. In all three countries, as in West Africa, the policy of 'one citizen, one vote' has been adopted, though both in Ceylon and in Pakistan some modifications were made in constituencies in order to achieve a balance of representation. What the consequences would have been in Pakistan we do not know, for a general election was never held. In Ceylon the devices used were only partially successful. Those of us who helped to frame the constitutional and electoral laws did not fully appreciate the strength of communalism among the illiterate and semi-literate electorate. We did provide for something like proportional representation of minorities, but we did not provide them with sufficient protection against communal legislation, and ambitious politicians made full use of their ability to appeal to the communal sentiments of the majority.

This is, however, a matter of detail. The essential question is whether it is practicable or desirable to limit the franchise for a fairly lengthy transitional period of, say, twenty years. As I have mentioned in chapter III, in the United Kingdom the franchise was extended slowly, over a period of roughly one hundred years. Clearly so long a period could not be contemplated in Africa, but a shorter period would have some advantages. First, while permitting a complete transfer of power forthwith, it would provide a longer period for the political education of the mass of the people. Indeed, the African politicians, knowing that in due course the franchise would be extended, would be compelled in their own interest to consider the needs of the masses and to secure their support. Secondly, a limited franchise, whatever form of limitation was adopted, would tend to keep out those who had had little or no education and who were more likely to think in local or tribal terms than in national terms. It might, therefore, prevent any equivalent of the appeal to communalism of which the Ceylonese politicians have made such use since 1956. Thirdly, in a multi-racial society, such as Kenya or the Rhodesias, a limited franchise would be the simplest way— though not the only way—of giving the economically more advanced sections of the population (usually Europeans and Asians) a larger share of political representation than their mere numbers would justify on the basis of counting heads. This would not only enable those whose collaboration for successful self-government is essential to accept such self-government more rapidly; it would also ensure that there would be no flight of capital, loss of sources of employment, or other interference with the economic progress of the territory.

There are, of course, arguments against a restricted franchise which would appeal especially to African politicians. First, they are anxious that African democracy should be the same as other democracies; that, of course, is impossible because other democracies are founded each on its own tradition; but at least the form can be the same, i.e. one citizen, one vote. Secondly, it has often been said that the people who need the franchise most are the under-privileged, because only through the ballot-box can they ensure attention to their needs, which are by definition greater than those of other people. There is sense in this argument, but the argument is double-edged. No electorate, not even an educated electorate, gets what it wants; it gets what politicians think it wants; and, since politicians want power, they support policies which will win votes in the short run, even if they are obviously disadvantageous in the long run. The sectionalism of which everybody complained in Pakistan, the communalism which has distressed Ceylon, and the communism which has racked Malaya, Singapore, Burma and Indonesia (among others) have been due to politicians capitalising the prejudices of people whose political education has lagged behind. It is not that they are illiterate, for literacy does not in itself lead to maturity of political judgment, though such judgment is more easily obtained by those who can and do read: it is that some experience of politics is required to distinguish between sound policies and unsound 'politics'. What the African elector usually wants is more land, and it is easy enough to promise him more land, though not so easy to provide it for him without subverting the economy of the country and depriving him of schools, medical services, roads and the general service of government.

Democracy in Africa

Finally, there is the argument which generally proves conclusive, though it is less frequently stressed than the others. The politicians of every country have something of the character of demagogues. They make 'party political' speeches, i.e. speeches which are intended to arouse the enthusiasm of their audiences. They do not put reasoned arguments before the electorate and ask the electors to choose. They decide what they think their audiences are likely to support and then appeal to prejudice with all the arts of oratory. It is easier to do that with an inexperienced electorate than it is with an experienced, and therefore rather cynical, electorate. The African politician who thus gets 'the people' behind him is in a strong position to achieve his ambitions—much stronger than any politician would be in Britain, because no British politician can ever say convincingly (though some say it unconvincingly) that he has 'the people' behind him. Hence the African politician is often prepared to 'trust the people' because he has been able to persuade the people to trust him. In a multi-racial society the argument is even stronger. To put it bluntly, the more Africans have votes, the more votes African politicians have at their disposal—until other African politicians come along and make even more attractive speeches.

The essential problem of African democracy is, I believe, the essential problem of democracy everywhere—and it is wise to remember that only a few countries in the world have really made a success of it. Democracy has succeeded in North-Western Europe and in a few countries outside Europe because it has become entwined in the traditions of the people. We know, almost by instinct, what matters are the concern of British politicians and what are not. We know because we have been brought up in the British tradition. If the Member for Cambridge dared to meddle with matters which, in our view, were no concern of his, it is pretty certain that enough of us would vote against him at the next election to make him lose his seat. We know, too, when he is talking reasonably and when he is talking 'party political'; and this is because we British electors and our fathers before us have heard party politicians orate for nearly two hundred years. We do not get many demagogues because we know the type; and any politician who tried to persuade us to a policy which would, in our view, create a run on the banks or an inflation of the currency

Change in Africa

would obtain less than one-eighth of the total votes polled and thus forfeit the £150 which he has to deposit before his nomination as a candidate can be accepted. British politicians, whatever political label they wear and whatever political party they support, have to adopt policies which look reasonable to a lot of reasonable people.

This kind of knowledge and experience will develop in Africa as elsewhere, but it takes time. The difficult period is, I think, that between the end of the first fine flush of enthusiasm for independence and the beginning of political maturity in the electorate at large. If there is a strong political organisation with its roots in the villages, and if the leadership is both efficient and honest, it may create an opposition to itself equally efficient and honest and so accustom the people generally to democratic ways. That is the hope, but it requires a series of favourable events. Among the obvious risks are nepotism and corruption; racialism, communalism or tribalism; dictatorship; anarchy or economic breakdown. These risks have to be taken by nationalist politicians, and they are usually taken rather light-heartedly because politicians everywhere tend to be convinced by their own oratory and to forget that they are politically mortal. There is no sure way of guarding against the risks. Constitutional safeguards help, but they can be overridden and in any case one must not impose too many restrictions on a developing country lest they hinder development. Through the United Nations and other organisations various kinds of assistance, which do not affect sovereignty, can be obtained. The main precaution is, however, a realisation that the risks do exist. In the burst of optimism which accompanies independence they are apt to be forgotten; and, indeed, those who take care to point out the risks are sometimes called 'anti-national' or even 'imperialist'. They are in fact public benefactors because they encourage ambitious politicians to study more carefully the way along which they are leading their people. The politicians are setting out on a journey into the unknown; enthusiasm and optimism are desirable qualities, but somebody has to take forethought to provide petrol and oil for the trucks and food and water for the men. 'Hasten slowly', says the Latin proverb, with that economy of words for which the Romans were famous.

VI. *Constitution-Making*

The drafting of a constitution is a technical job which, like other technical jobs, is best done by those with experience of it. Fortunately, the most experienced of the technicians are the legal staff of the Colonial Office, whose services are available to colonies on the way to independence. Where it is thought impracticable or undesirable to rely exclusively on these distinguished lawyers, there are plenty of others available.

A draftsman must, however, have instructions, for the essential principles of a constitution require political decisions. What is more, the political decisions ought to relate to the peculiar conditions of the territory to which the constitution is intended to apply. The French lawyers sought to provide a common legal framework, to which separate provisions relating to the particular territory could be attached. The constitutions within the Commonwealth have tended to follow a pattern because there has been so much borrowing from the British Constitution; but English lawyers and colonial politicians prefer to think out each problem afresh. The pattern is reproduced because, considering the problems of the territory and the experience of its people under British rule, it seems desirable to copy the pattern, with such modifications as will suit local conditions. This is because every territory has its own constitutional history, even in Africa, where the British connection has usually been much shorter than in Asia or the West Indies. In fact, what usually happens is that the colonial politicians sit down with the Governor or the Chief Secretary and their respective legal advisers to work out what proposals they shall lay before the Secretary of State. A deputation then leaves for London, where the Secretary of State and his advisers, the Governor and his advisers, and the colonial politicians and their advisers, sit round a table to try to work out an agreed scheme. The agreed scheme is then worked into a draft Constitution by the legal advisers to the

Constitution-making

Secretary of State. It is circulated for discussion and is examined by the Governor and his advisers and by the colonial politicians and their advisers. Often agreement can be reached by correspondence; but if that is impracticable another meeting has to be held, so that a reasonably agreed constitution can be put into operation by Her Majesty in Council.

This process seems simple, but it is not always so simple as it appears, because the colonial politicians are not necessarily agreed among themselves. The constitution which will ultimately emerge will regulate the government of the territory not merely for the next five years, but for a very long time. This is particularly true where it represents a compromise among political or communal groups, because then it will be necessary to make amendment rather difficult, in order that minority views may be protected. Clauses which a minority insists on having put in are useless if, the day after independence, the majority can simply have them removed. Sometimes it is provided that certain provisions shall not be capable of amendment, or shall not be capable of amendment within ten or twenty years, or shall not be capable of amendment except by a two-thirds majority in the legislature, or shall not be capable of amendment except by an absolute majority in each of the two Houses of the legislature, or shall not be capable of amendment except after a referendum, or something of that kind. In any case, the local politicians have to remember that the constitution will apply not only to them, but also to their successors; and their successors may be their political opponents. A constitution always looks very different to politicians in opposition from what it looks to politicians in power. What are called 'checks and balances' often appear to the politicians in power to be unnecessary restrictions on their freedom to prescribe what is necessary in the interests of the country; when the same politicians move into opposition the same checks and balances often seem to be wise limitations on the power of the government to play fast and loose with the interest of the country.

It is important to remember, too, that the success of a constitution depends very largely on the strength of the support given to it by the people. I have already emphasised that the social and economic order depends upon the confidence of the people. Whoever is in power will of course want to change the social and economic order, to make it better by legislation; but the effectiveness of that legislation depends upon the extent to which it is acceptable. The first step, therefore, is to make the legislature acceptable, so that people can follow the lead which the legislature gives them. What we want them to say is, 'This is an Act of Parliament; therefore we ought to do our best to make it effective', not 'This is another piece of interference by those rotten politicians; how can we evade it?' Hence, both because the constitution may last for a very long time and because it is necessary to give it popular support, it ought to be based, so far as may be practicable, on general agreement. Examples (not all from the Commonwealth) will show the various methods of reaching agreement.

In the case of Ghana, the Secretary of State himself negotiated a compromise, though it did not last very long because it was not adequately protected in the constitution and the provisions desired by the Ashanti were removed. The problem was appreciated. It was provided in the constitution that there should be a two-thirds majority in the National Assembly for any constitutional amendment, and that certain kinds of constitutional amendments should require in addition the support of two-thirds of the Regional Assemblies. These and other precautions proved inadequate because, as experience elsewhere has since demonstrated, the first election is likely to produce a large majority for the party which secures independence. If the Regional Assemblies had been set up before independence, the result might have been different. If some of the constitutional provisions had been protected for ten years they might have been protected for all time. Even so, it is easy to be wise after the event. The detailed provisions of the Ghanaian Constitution seemed to be adequate at the time at which they were drafted.

In the case of the Maldive Islands the draft constitution was submitted to a referendum and was approved, though subsequent economic difficulties, and inexpert handling of them, caused the constitution to be overthrown less than a year later. In Ceylon, the Ministers tried to produce a compromise constitution which would, they believed, be accepted by the minorities. After it had been approved, with modifications, by the Secretary of State, they submitted to the legislature a resolution that it be approved, and it was approved

Constitution-making

by a very large majority. In India and Pakistan temporary constitutions were provided in order that permanent constitutions might be worked out by representative constituent assemblies. India succeeded in getting a generally agreed constitution in three years. It subsequently required a good deal of amendment, though such amendment was possible because of the dominance of the Congress party. Pakistan's first draft, which took seven years to formulate, was a complete failure. The second draft took less than two years, though it never came fully into operation.

In Nepal, the King appointed a small representative commission, which produced a draft constitution. This was submitted to a representative assembly appointed by the King and approved. In Singapore it was decided to send an all-party delegation to London to negotiate with the Secretary of State. Though it failed at its first attempt, it made sufficient progress to succeed at the second attempt. This was one of the rare cases in which the result of the next election could not be forecast. In Malaya, on the other hand, the Alliance formed by Tunku Abdul Rahman already had an immense majority. Even so, the constitutional problem was so difficult, because of the competing interests of the Malays, the Chinese and the Indians, that the Secretary of State was asked to appoint a Commission consisting of persons nominated by the Governments of the United Kingdom, Canada, Australia, India and Pakistan (though the Canadian did not serve). With some modifications, the Commission's recommendations were accepted both by the United Kingdom and by Malaya. In Nigeria most of the constitutional provisions were worked out by agreement at all-party conferences with the Secretary of State, but certain matters in acute controversy were left to independent commissions.

It will be seen that nearly every case is peculiar, the reason being that there is always a background of competing interests. The framing of a constitution for an independent country is really only the latest step in constitutional development, and before that step is taken some aspects of the development become clear. For instance, it was clear that India, Pakistan, Malaya and Nigeria had to be federations, though it was not clear how the Settlements (Penang and Malacca) were to be fitted into the Malayan Federation nor how many Regions there should be in the Nigerian Federation. In Malaya there were already nine states with separate Rulers to whom their Malay subjects were most loyal and also two colonies which had to be taken over. It was therefore necessary to retain the states even though the country as a whole was small. In Nigeria the country was large and the people diverse both in respect of religion and in respect of tribe and language. Federations are expensive and difficult to run, and sometimes, as in the Republic of South Africa and in Ghana (under the initial constitution) it is possible to have wide devolution of powers without depriving the central legislature of its over-riding power. On the other hand, a federation may be the only means of enabling a diversity of people to govern themselves.

These questions are usually settled at an early stage. As I have already emphasised in chapter V, there are sound reasons for making the development towards independence as gradual as possible. Unfortunately nationalist politicians bid against each other in the hope of attracting support for themselves. If one says 'independence as soon as possible' another says 'within five years', and then a third says 'immediately' and a fourth says 'now'. Since neither 'immediately' nor 'now' (if there is any difference) is in fact practicable, this is like trying to kill a wild boar with a rubber spear. It is even impossible to fix dates until all the major questions have been settled. One can hardly quote the Belgian Congo, because no British territory is so backward and no British Government would have acted so irresponsibly. It is, however, an extreme case of hasty abdication. If a territory is to have a good chance of a successful career as an independent state, it must set out on that career with its major problems solved for the time being. The time taken depends on the difficulty of the problems and especially on competing claims. This is the reason for using different methods to solve them and for taking the solution in at least two stages. In the first the British Government retains control but as far as possible powers are delegated to African Ministers. The Ministers learn their jobs, the civil servants get used to working with them, and the people as a whole get used to the process of self-government, so that there is no loss of confidence when British control is withdrawn. Meanwhile the Secretary of State, the Governor, and the local politicians can work out the constitutional

Constitution-making

principles so as to give instructions to draftsmen, and agree upon the terms of the draft constitution. A date for independence can then be fixed in the Order in Council enacting the constitution.

The problems to be solved are numerous. They are more numerous than colonial politicians are usually aware of, because their fundamental interest is in the transfer of power from the British Government to themselves, whereas the draftsmen and the Colonial Office are more interested in securing a constitution which will function efficiently, both now and in the future. The following are some of the more *important* questions to be settled.

1. Monarchy or Republic?

This question is far less important than is commonly supposed. There are minor differences of form, and the difficulties of drafting a republican constitution are greater, partly because provision has to be made for the election, resignation and removal of the President, and partly because executive powers have to be defined more carefully than when they are simply those of the Crown. One advantage of the monarchy is that it provides for continuity in theory, while allowing a complete transfer of responsibility in fact. The monarchy therefore helps to maintain confidence. What is more, a good Governor-General can, by wise advice, help the newly independent country through its initial difficulties while the politicians are still inexperienced—as Lord Elgin did in Canada over a hundred years ago. On the other hand, the Indian politicians felt compelled to decide for a republic in 1950 because the Crown had so long been associated with British rule. Pakistan followed in 1956 because India had become a republic. The Ghanaian politicians had a different reason, that the villager was not convinced of the reality of independence until an African became Head of the State. In fact, however, wider powers have been conferred on the President of Ghana than those vested in the President of the Union of India, and so we may doubt if this was the real reason.

2. Federation or Unitary State?

Something has been said on this subject already. A country would not have a federal constitution if it could avoid it, because such a constitution is necessarily complicated and expensive. The powers of government have to be divided between the federation and the states, there have to be several legislatures and governments instead of one of each, separate staffs, estimates and systems of taxation. In other words, a country which is short of personnel of high quality has to set up several administrative machines. Also, no federal machine works without considerable friction. On the other hand, a federal constitution may be a reasonable compromise between those who think in national terms and those who think in regional or sectional terms. There are, of course, other methods, as the United Kingdom (i.e. England, Wales, Scotland and Northern Ireland) and the Republic of South Africa show. Also there are very great variations among the federations in the Commonwealth—Canada, Australia, India, Pakistan, Malaya and Nigeria—and the United States of America provide another precedent.

3. Unicameral or Bicameral Legislature?

Most central legislatures in the Commonwealth consist of two Houses, following the example of the United Kingdom. The advantages and disadvantages of a Second Chamber cannot be discussed in general terms, for they depend entirely on the conditions in the country concerned. The arguments for a Second Chamber in the United Kingdom would not apply to Malaya. In most Commonwealth countries the strongest argument for a Second Chamber is, however, the diversity of the people. If the extreme nationalist view be adopted for the First Chamber, so that one seat be provided for every 75,000 or 100,000 inhabitants, the result may be far from a fair representation of the people. A Christian or a Muslim minority, or an important tribal minority, or a European or an Asian minority, or indeed any significant minority, may be completely unrepresented because there is no constituency in which it has a majority. Alternatively, though the minorities are spread throughout the country, their seats may be localised because of their distribution. Minority X may have seats in Region A but not in Region B; minority Y may have seats in Region B but none in Region A. Since Region A may differ substantially from Region B because of its superior natural

Constitution-making

resources, this sort of representation may be inadequate; for in that case Region *A* would produce most of the revenue and Region *B* would require much of the expenditure.

There may indeed be no majority at all because each of three or four regions is dominated by a distinct minority. This fact may not be evident at the outset, for politicians from different minorities may combine or coalesce in order to achieve independence and then break up because of their personal ambitions or of pressure from their own communities. The alliance of Malays, Chinese and Indians in the Federation of Malaya depends very largely on the public spirit of a few nationalist leaders. There is a tendency for the extreme Malays and the extreme Chinese to break away from the leadership of the moderate men who achieved power in 1957.

Attempts to solve these problems may be made by careful manipulation of the franchise and the constituencies. The advantage of a Second Chamber is that it enables an alternative method of representation to be devised. In a federation, for instance, there may be representation by population in the First Chamber and representation by states in the Second Chamber, as in the United States. There each state has representation in the House of Representatives in proportion to its population, but every state has equal representation in the Senate. This is one of the simplest forms of double representation: there are many other forms. In any case the question of powers is inevitably raised, particularly because, in the British system which most Commonwealth countries adopt, the Government is responsible to the legislature. It is not impossible to have responsibility to both Chambers, and the first draft constitution of Pakistan was drafted on such an assumption. On the other hand, it is very much easier, both for purposes of drafting and for purposes of actual working (though we have no experience of the latter) if there is responsibility to the First Chamber only. The draftsmen have then to ask themselves what is to happen if the Government is able to get its legislative proposals through the First Chamber but they are rejected in the Second Chamber. In the United Kingdom, as we have seen, the House of Commons can override the House of Lords, but the latter cannot claim to be a representative Second Chamber. Elsewhere, some other device, such as a joint meeting of both

Chambers, or a general election for both Chambers, or an enlarged majority in the First Chamber, has to be adopted.

4. Representation

Representation is a subject on which it is possible to say very little in general terms, because the problem varies so much from territory to territory. There is a tendency among both Asian and African politicians to choose the British system, i.e. adult franchise with roughly equal single-member constituencies or 'one person, one vote, one value'. One reason for this preference is that in a multi-racial society it always favours the majority, from which the politicians are usually drawn. There is, however, the general argument that the British system is more 'democratic'. That, I think, is a misunderstanding. It is certainly a convenient way of giving representation to the British people; but they are a homogeneous people organised in an individualist society; and, as I have explained in chapter III, even they modify the principle of 'one person, one vote, one value' in practice. Also, they recognise that their system does not produce proportional representation even of political opinion. It encourages the two-party system and exaggerates the government's majority. These consequences are probably an advantage, but they would not necessarily be so in other countries, particularly in a multi-racial society in which the system would probably benefit the largest of the communities. In a country like Ceylon it is certainly desirable to balance the communal representation, and even to provide by nomination for the representation of small communities which could not secure election by nomination. Communal electorates, the reservation of seats for particular communities, communal 'primaries', and other devices worked out in Asia between 1932 and 1947 have both advantages and disadvantages. A balance between villagers and townsfolk is struck in many democratic countries. Though most methods of proportional representation require a literate electorate, there are less refined forms which can be used with an illiterate electorate. In short the problem of representation ought to be considered afresh for every territory, given the nature of the population and its social system or systems. For most African territories this is the most difficult of all the problems of constitutional drafting because behind it is the problem

Constitution-making

of political power. Whatever system of representation be adopted, it will benefit one group of politicians in the short run, while another system of representation will benefit another group. This is so whether the divisions among the population are tribal, religious or 'racial'—i.e. among Africans, Asians and Europeans. The largest 'community' almost inevitably stands out for representation by population; but by doing so it frightens other 'communities' by a fear of 'communal' legislation—and Asian experience does not suggest that the fear is misplaced. If agreement is reached, it is generally as a result of hard bargaining in which little thought is given to the remoter future, when the present generation of politicians will be names in the history books.

In such conditions it is difficult to say anything helpful except to make the purely negative suggestion, as I have done already in chapter V, that a straightforward copying of the British system—without a House of Lords—is usually the least satisfactory method of dealing with the problem because the conditions in Britain are so utterly different. The problem of representation deserves professional study by advisers before it is tossed into political competition. The politicians may not agree with the advisers, but at least they will be given some ideas in which purely political and personal exigencies play no part.

5. Protective clauses

It is unlikely that the problem of representation will be solved to everybody's satisfaction. The most that can be hoped for is a reasonable compromise of competing claims. In the long run democracy implies some form of majority rule: but it is precisely majority rule which minorities generally fear. For them it may be the wrong majority, or a majority dominated by the wrong ideas. It may therefore be thought desirable to introduce clauses by which even the majority will be bound. The simplest form of such clauses prevents legislation which discriminates on the ground of religion, tribe, 'race' or other community, as in Ceylon. The most complicated is a Bill of Rights with full provision for legal remedies if any of the rights are infringed, as in India. For the draftsmen these are difficult provisions because they will apply to conditions which the draftsmen cannot foresee. Let us take as an example one of the simplest of 'fundamental liberties', freedom of speech. Clearly there can be no democracy without freedom of speech, and the first step taken by any dictator, fascist, military or communist, is to suppress it. On the other hand, everybody knows that freedom of speech must be qualified: one cannot allow complete freedom to defame other people, to incite to violence, to start rebellion, or to induce chaos. As soon as one begins to draft qualifications, however, difficulties arise. There are exceptional circumstances in which, as any democrat would agree, even censorship is justified, but nobody can define beforehand what those circumstances are. In the same way there have to be limitations on all 'fundamental liberties', because liberty to create anarchy or to start rebellion or to induce rioting is not liberty but unjustifiable licence. Personally, I prefer the very general type of 'fundamental liberty', but it necessarily uses vague language which has to be interpreted, and perhaps reinterpreted, from generation to generation. It is, however, difficult for politicians who expect to have a majority to accept broad and uncertain limitations on the power which they expect to exercise; and it is equally difficult for politicians who expect to be in a minority to accept vague formulae which may or may not give them the protection that they think they require. Most Bills of Rights are therefore compromises between the broad generalisations of the American Bill of Rights (which have been interpreted in a long series of judgments of the Supreme Court of the United States) and the more detailed Bill of Rights in the Indian constitution. Either type leads inevitably to a good deal of litigation unless it is expressly prevented, as in the constitution of the Federation of Malaya.

There are, however, other types of protective clauses. One way to satisfy minority opinion, be it racial, religious or tribal, is to find out exactly what it is that the minorities fear. If they fear discrimination in appointments to the public service or the judiciary, it is possible to provide for the making of appointments by impartial and non-political commissions. If they fear that they will be required to learn and use the language of the majority it is possible to protect the minority languages either nationally or locally. If they fear that schools will be used to propagate the religion of the majority, it is

Constitution-making

possible to protect denominational schools or to forbid religious teaching in state schools. If they fear that the powers of their chiefs will be undermined, it is possible to fit the chiefs into the constitutional structure. These are examples only. Nearly all the devices adopted have a common disadvantage. Protective clauses usually protect things as they are—the *status quo*; but things will be different in fifty years' time. The protective clauses of one generation often look ridiculous, and may even be thought obstructive, two generations later. Even so, they are necessary to give a constitution popular support; and one can always hope that, after the clauses have become obsolete, they can be removed by substantial agreement.

VII. *The Aftermath*

A constitution is but a means to an end; and the end is good government. The quality of government depends upon the people who exercise it, not upon the constitution. One could, for instance, have Government and Parliament functioning in the best manner and form of Whitehall and Westminster, and yet have the country sinking rapidly to depression and perhaps anarchy developing. Prophecies of woe have so often come from opposition benches that it has been said that there is 'a good deal of ruination in a nation'. That is particularly true of Africa, because a stable agricultural population, engaged mainly in production for subsistence, is little concerned with policies of government. An industrial society, on the other hand, is dependent upon economic policy in respect of currency, credit, trade, taxation and so forth. An industrial economy is less stable than an agricultural economy, because nobody can eat pressed steel, concrete blocks, television sets or nylon stockings; these thing have to be sold in order to buy the things to eat and drink; and it has to be done through a complicated economic system which is easily disrupted by governmental policy. Nevertheless, it is essential to remember that politicians can as easily do harm as they can do good. They have behind them the knowledge and experience of the public service; but in a new state that knowledge and experience may not be very great. What is more, the public service can do no more than advise and warn: the decisions have to be taken by the politicians. Their task is both difficult and highly responsible; they deserve both support and sympathy. On the other hand, it is almost as easy for a politician to make mistakes in public affairs as it is for an ordinary citizen to make mistakes in his private affairs. He has better advice, but he is dealing with more difficult problems and the consequences of error are more far-reaching. Those who approach the task of decision with appropriate humility—not, however, a normal characteristic of a politician—will

The Aftermath

know that they are being asked to decide on inadequate information and will tend to procrastinate. Those who drive their trucks with their eyes on their passengers are likely to end in the ditch. The experienced politician develops a sort of intuition which enables him to choose between decision and procrastination, and between one decision and another. He is not always right, but he is not very often very wrong. Only time can give such experience.

It is much easier to run a governmental machine than to develop new policies. Unless the working of the machine has been seriously obstructed by nationalist agitation—as it was in India in 1947—British officials hand over an efficient machine in good running order; and, as I have already emphasised, sufficient delay is usually imposed to enable African politicians to take it over and run it without loss of confidence. On the other hand, no politician is content just to run the machine. His pre-independence propaganda has laid stress on the advantages which, he says, independence will bring to the electorate; the electorate expects him to take steps to secure those advantages; and the members of the legislature will want him to enable them to carry out their election pledges so that they can get re-elected at the next election. Ambitious development plans are politically inevitable. One need not be a hide-bound conservative to realise that all development plans contain an element of imagination, prophecy, guess-work —call it what you will—and therefore an element of risk. Indeed, it is usually found that experts differ in their forecasts, and that politicians and their advisers have to decide matters on which experts disagree. Politicians usually get praised when their schemes are ambitious and imaginative. They therefore tend to overrule or discount pessimistic forecasts. They ought, of course, to be praised when their inspired guesses prove to be correct. But when eggs are laid by hens which came from the eggs which were laid by the hens which the politicians imported, the politicians are usually dead or in honourable retirement. All this is, of course, as true in Europe as in Africa; and indeed British politicians have been known to produce singularly unsuccessful development plans for emergent Africa, though they have also produced plans which have helped Africa to emerge. The difficulty is that African politicians are forced by political, social and economic conditions to produce ambitious plans forthwith. Indeed, an African politician who was not anxious to produce plans to reduce the appalling poverty in which so many Africans have to live would be a traitor to his fellow-men.

This is not, however, the only problem. The new states of Africa have a part to play in the international scene. They are members of the United Nations. They have to take part in international diplomacy. Of these things an African politician cannot be expected to have more than a superficial knowledge, since until independence external affairs are matters for the Government of the United Kingdom. He will, of course, find plenty of people willing to advise him. If his country remains within the Commonwealth, he will receive the confidential communications which Commonwealth Governments send to each other; the High Commissioner in London will send information about the personal consultations which take place there; he will, in due course, attend the Prime Ministers' Conferences in London. Since the representatives of Commonwealth countries do not have to agree, and do not in fact agree on many subjects, these consultations permit of the study of different points of view. A similar educative process follows from the debates and private discussions at the United Nations.

There are, however, many others glad to help. All the great states, and many others, will want to exchange ambassadors or ministers, and each of them will be anxious to put the point of view adopted by his country's government. It is an over-simplification to say that these points of view are western, communist and 'uncommitted'. Any African State which adopts a democratic system is committed, since it is the main purpose of communist policy to overthrow democratic institutions. A fascist or military dictatorship must inevitably break up because no dictator can last more than one generation, though a party dictatorship may possibly last two or three generations. A democracy can certainly last for centuries and may last for all time. Those who are bred to a communist ideology therefore recognise that democracy is the principal enemy of communism. This does not imply, however, that communist governments will forthwith adopt an unfriendly attitude. On the contrary, it may be tactically wise for them to protest friendship, in the hope that opportunities will be given for subversive activity in Africa and that wedges can be driven

The Aftermath

between the African State and other democratic states. Nor does the antagonism between communism and democracy imply that an African country must follow the line of policy adopted by other democratic states. On the contrary, democracy postulates differences of opinion, both within a democratic state and among democratic states. The policies of democratic states are not likely to be consistent because democracy implies that differences of opinion will produce different policies. Indeed, it is by no means certain that communist dictatorships will always produce consistent policies. Leninism was not identical with Marxism, Stalinism was not identical with Leninism, and Stalinism has been discredited in the Soviet Union. Except in Yugoslavia and Albania, the power, influence and ruthlessness of the Soviet Union has hitherto kept communist parties to the Soviet party line, even when it changed (though in the democratic countries, where it is possible even for communists to have minds of their own, they have lost many members in the process—in the United Kingdom, for instance, the ex-communists are more numerous than the communists). The conversion of China into a great communist power has, however, produced an evident divergence between Russian-inspired and Chinese-inspired communism.

If these questions related solely to ideology they would be comparatively unimportant. Communist strategy and even tactics are fairly obvious on the international plane, and African politicians are not likely to be deceived by them. It is indeed doubtful if the politicians who flirt with communist parties are always deceived. They often take risks with their eyes open. The difficulty in Africa is the urgent need of capital to finance the ambitious development schemes which are thought necessary to raise the standard of living. Nearly the whole of that capital must come from countries which can afford to divert it from their own needs to those of Africa. These must be, in present conditions, the United States, the Soviet Union, the United Kingdom, France and Western Germany.

Inside the communist *bloc* there is no philanthropy which has not a political motive. This is indeed part of communist ideology. If a Russian grant or loan is offered, it must have a political purpose. It is commonly said by African politicians that they will take money from anywhere if it is offered 'without strings'. They mean by this that no conditions are attached to the gift or the loan. In the case of Russian gifts and loans there always are 'strings' even if they are for the time being invisible. An outright gift of aircraft, trucks or other equipment may appear to have no strings, but in fact it has. Such equipment has to be serviced either by Russian technicians or by local technicians trained in Russia. Russian technicians are not employees of private industry, as British or American technicians are: they are government employees subject to orders, and they are invariably used for political purposes. I have myself been employed in technical assistance to under-developed countries, both on behalf of the United Nations and on behalf of the United Kingdom. I have never received orders from either: my services have simply been placed at the disposal of the government of the country concerned. I am a private citizen and a member of a very independent profession: if the government of the United Kingdom tried to use me as a political instrument, I should refuse the job and publicly explain why. But I am a free citizen of a free country: no Russian citizen can claim such independence.

Further, if technicians are sent to the United States or the United Kingdom for training, they are simply sent to spend some weeks or months with a private firm having the particular knowledge and skill required. Any 'ideologies' they pick up come from newspapers and talks with fellow-workers. It is nobody's business to teach them 'the American way of life' or the principles of the British Constitution. They can, if they like, say that they are all a lot of nonsense. They may in fact find themselves working with communists who can and do say that these things are a lot of nonsense. If technicians are sent to Russia, however, they have to go to government factories in which indoctrination in communist ideology is part of the day's work; and if any fellow-worker were to dare to say that communism was a lot of nonsense both would find themselves in gaol. In other words a Russian offer of technical assistance will inevitably lead to political propaganda, either through the use of Russian experts for that purpose or by the indoctrination of local experts. Naturally these devices do not always succeed: but the important point is that the fundamental purpose of the offer is political.

Finally, Russian equipment requires Russian spares, which can be purchased only from the Russian Government. The Russian

The Aftermath

Government can then attach as many 'strings' as it thinks fit, for the African Government will hesitate to render its equipment useless by not being able to replace parts worn or damaged. On the other hand, American or British equipment is made by private companies whose only ambition is to sell their products. Spares can be bought on the open market as easily as cigarettes or soap, and with as little political danger.

I do not mean to suggest that American or British technical assistance is entirely free from political motives. The dominant purpose is philanthropic or humanitarian. In Britain it is reinforced by the sense of responsibility towards other members of the Commonwealth. In the United States it is reinforced by the sense of responsibility which so many Americans feel towards people less well-endowed than themselves. Nevertheless, the Governments of the United States and the United Kingdom, in their different fashions (the British, for instance, less blatantly than the American), do not hesitate to advertise any technical or other assistance that they may give. They hope that, if it proves successful, it will help to cement good relations with Africa. Such help is, of course, very indirect. It is simply a small part of a lengthy diplomatic process.

The 'cold war' is not, however, the only aspect of international relations with which a new African State must be concerned. It is the fashion in all countries to adopt a 'holier than thou' attitude: that is, to think that, if only other people behaved like us, the world would be a better place. This is as noticeable in Asia as it is in Europe or America. The 'image' which India projects, for instance, depends whether it is seen by Indians, Pakistanis, or Ceylonese. Phrases like 'power politics' are misleading slogans, invented to suggest that somebody else's policies are less moral than one's own. Some politicians are more cynical than others—I should, for instance, draw a sharp distinction between Mr Kruschev and Mr Nehru, though both have a genuine belief in the doctrines which they use to lecture the rest of us. But all politicians are concerned with their own and their countries' prestige. So long as there are independent states there will be international competition: and sometimes (especially in unstable dictatorships) politicians have to appear to win in the international competition in order to keep themselves in power. There is no reason for supposing that Africa will be free from this international competition. On the contrary, there are signs of it in West Africa, by no means limited to what used to be British West Africa. In East Africa there are, as yet, fewer new states; but there are in Egypt and the Sudan unstable dictatorships either of which might topple if it sustained a rousing diplomatic defeat.

There are thus plenty of international problems facing the new States of Africa. Even so, I think that their fundamental problems are internal. It will take time for them to develop the internal cohesion which older countries have long since attained. It will come about, as it is doing in Asia, as the new generation repudiates ancestral loyalties and antipathies. A Nigerian schoolboy will become less of a Yoruba or an Ibo and more of a Nigerian, than his father. What is needed meanwhile is political stability. Democratic government is a difficult process because it relies so much on the good faith of ambitious politicians who are subject to a good many temptations. If the leaders spurn the temptation to abuse their power, they are likely to have followers who will not. Even in India, which has had excellent leadership for nearly fifteen years, there are plenty of allegations of corruption at the lower levels. In countries like Turkey, Pakistan, Iraq, Egypt and the Sudan, corruption has been alleged as a justification for military rule—though there is no reason to suppose that military officers, if they rule long enough, are less susceptible to corruption than politicians.

Even more dangerous is the possibility that, until internal cohesion develops, politicians will use sectional differences to keep themselves in, or to attain, power. One could not blame an African electorate, any more than one can blame an Asian electorate, for possessing ideas and emotions which have been handed down from generation to generation. Indeed, British administrators have fostered local traditions in order to make government easier by 'indirect rule'. The change to independence does not automatically cause ancestral loyalties to disintegrate. It would be surprising if ambitious politicians did not make use of them. What is more, as we have already seen, political propaganda before independence fosters the impression that independence will immediately improve social and economic conditions, though any such improvement will be narrowly limited to classes which are already favoured.

The Aftermath

It is necessary to understand these difficulties in order that they may be overcome. African political leaders have the same defects as political leaders in other countries. On the other hand, they have the same devotion to the public good and the same ambition to improve the lot of their fellow-men. As a student of government who has been much concerned in finding solutions to the difficult problems which they have to face, I have tried to explain quite frankly what those difficulties are. Solutions can be helped by constitutional devices, but their success depends essentially on the men and women who give them effect. The first twenty years of self-government is inevitably a difficult period; but there is no problem that cannot be solved by people who are energetic, imaginative and devoted servants of their fellow-men.

For EU product safety concerns, contact us at Calle de José Abascal, 56–1º,
28003 Madrid, Spain or eugpsr@cambridge.org.

www.ingramcontent.com/pod-product-compliance
Ingram Content Group UK Ltd.
Pitfield, Milton Keynes, MK11 3LW, UK
UKHW041420180426
11947UKWH00007B/225